Father Kemp

Father Kemp and his old folks:

a history of the old folks' concerts : comprising an autobiography of the author and

sketches of many humorous scenes and incidents which have transpired in a

concert-giving experience of twelve years in America and England

Father Kemp

Father Kemp and his old folks:
a history of the old folks' concerts : comprising an autobiography of the author and sketches of many humorous scenes and incidents which have transpired in a concert-giving experience of twelve years in America and England

ISBN/EAN: 9783741158261

Manufactured in Europe, USA, Canada, Australia, Japa

Cover: Foto ©Andreas Hilbeck / pixelio.de

Manufactured and distributed by brebook publishing software
(www.brebook.com)

Father Kemp

Father Kemp and his old folks:

Father Kemp and his Old Folks.

A HISTORY

OF THE

OLD FOLKS' CONCERTS,

COMPRISING AN

AUTOBIOGRAPHY OF THE AUTHOR,

AND SKETCHES OF MANY HUMOROUS SCENES AND INCIDENTS, WHICH
HAVE TRANSPIRED IN A CONCERT-GIVING EXPERIENCE OF
TWELVE YEARS IN AMERICA AND ENGLAND.

BOSTON:
PUBLISHED BY THE AUTHOR.
1869.

PREFACE.

IT is a great undertaking to write even a small book. Every one has an object in placing himself before the public in print. What my object is, will gradually develop itself at I proceed with my story. I was always ambitious. Not an office within the‚ gift of the American people has been at times above my aspirations. My tastes have varied, — sometimes with the weather, sometimes with my business successes and reverses, — but, generally speaking, had I been nominated for any political position, I should have thrown aside every consideration of personal reputation, and blindly accepted — for the good of the Republic. But I must say it was never one of my early ambitions to make a book.

The reader will, of course, desire to know when the mortal coil which contains such an ardent and self-sacrificing nature was first flung from the ship of time, and where it dropped. It landed on Cape Cod — the home of brave, sturdy hearts, and sand — perhaps a hundred years ago — perhaps less; at least, long enough ago to enable me to become acquainted with the manners, customs, and personal appearance of those but a generation removed from the Mayflower's precious cargo. I hope the reader will consider the question of time an unimportant one; the period of my birth has always been kept a matter of profound secrecy, and only those who have attended the "Old Folks' Concerts" have an approximate idea of my venerable appearance and precise age.

In political matters I have held many different opinions. Living through so many years, with changes frequently occurring in the aspects of the country's institutions, I of course changed with the times; but I venture to say that within the past hundred years of my life I have not done more, in that respect, than many, whom the people have preferred before me, have accomplished in ten years. I wish now that my political opinions had undergone more frequent revolutions. I think, if they had, I should by this time be at least a Member of Congress.

My lot has been a different one from what my early, and even later, aspirations marked out. However unromantic it may seem, reader, I am a shoe-dealer. "Everybody suited at No. 794 Washington St.," is my motto. This, however, is not mentioned as an advertisement. I would scorn to harbor such an intention in a publication which, I hope, will be purely of a literary, and not a business, character. But, at the same time, should the reader see fit to drop in at No. 794, he will at all seasons find a good stock, and a determination on my part to sell.

My experience as the conductor of more than six thousand Old Folks' Concerts, given in many parts of America, and in England, has enabled me to collect some facts, and to witness many ludicrous incidents, all of which cannot, of course, be mentioned in this volume; but I will endeavor to write down a few, in my own way, giving a history of an enterprise which, I take just pride in saying, was originated by me. I do not ask you to "pity the sorrows of a poor old man" because there have been many weak imitations of the "Old Folks' Concerts." The imitators got the worst of it, — at least, so everybody said. The entertainments could not be copyrighted, any more than the report of a cannon could be; consequently, numerous "original Father Kemps" have imposed themselves upon the credulous public, many of whom, as I hear, have excelled in drinking whiskey, cheating landlords, and showing that they were "fathers" of mischief and dishonesty as well as conductors of choirs which sung religious music. Such evils are, in my case, not the penalties of greatness, but the results of success. Therefore, when I am introduced to a person who invites me to join him in a drink, declaring he shouldn't have known me *again*, I had so changed since we last met in private, I conclude, after refusing his invitation, that some of my venerable imitators have " smiled " with him, after the Concert given by the " original Father Kemp and his troupe of Old Folks." One of my objects in giving this volume to the public is to let them know that *the* original F. K. is at No. 794 Washington St., and that he neither drinks with the acquaintances of his hoary-headed namesakes, nor satisfies the demands of their creditors.

This book will contain a history of the " Old Folks' Concerts " which originated in the vicinity of Boston, and in the course of twelve years obtained a world-wide reputation. Some of the incidents narrated may seem silly, as they doubtlessly are; and if the reader wishes to find fault because they are in print, let him console himself that I know of hundreds of others, far more silly, which happened in my experience.

I am under great obligations to the Pilgrim Fathers for landing so near Cape Cod. I thank them heartily. Had they gone farther South, their descendants would have dressed differently, sung different psalm-tunes, I might have been somebody else, and, consequently, " Father Kemp " would never have had a chance in the world. Everything has happened just right for me, and it is hoped the Pilgrims will not suffer from anything that has occurred. In thus speaking of the Plymouth Pilgrims, no slight is intended to the Puritans of the Massachusetts colony, many of whose descendants were members of my choir.

After so many years of active contact with the world, it is a grateful privilege to have a place where rest and quiet can be found, and where one can meet his friends, and feel, in his old age, that he may repay them for years of kindness, if they do as he desires. Such are my thoughts, when I contemplate the cheap rates at which my goods are held; and friends, I am confident, appreciate my motives in laboring so assiduously for their advantage. Notwithstanding the publication of this book, they will still find me at No. 794 Washington Street.

FATHER KEMP.

Boston, March, 1868.

CONTENTS.

—◦◦◦—

CHAPTER I.

CHAPTER II.

CHAPTER III.

CHAPTER VIII.

CHAPTER IX.

CHAPTER X.

CHAPTER XI.

CHAPTER XII.

CHAPTER XIII.

CHAPTER XIV.

CHAPTER XV.

CHAPTER XVI.

CHAPTER XVII.

FATHER KEMP AND HIS OLD FOLKS.

CHAPTER I.

A Little Seafaring Experience — Change of Occupation and Mode of Living — Farm in Reading — Agricultural Experience — Fancy Farming, and how much it Costs — The Hen-Fever — Profits on Apples, Potatoes, ahd Squashes — The Origin of the Old Folks' Concerts — My Neighbors.

IT has been intimated in the preface that I was born on Cape Cod. That occurrence will explain how, at the age of nine years, I found myself aboard a Cape Cod pinkey boat, which was commanded by my uncle, occupying the position of cook for twelve men. We were bound on a fishing cruise. I felt the dignity of the new office, and was bound to maintain it. I went to work with a will. While the rest of the crew, having got the vessel safely out of the port, were lounging about, with no cares save to smoke their pipes and "chaff," I was in the cabin, busily employed in preparing the first dinner, which I was determined should be a credit to the youthful cook. When we got outside, there was quite a heavy sea

11

on, and the roll of the craft of course affected the
cooking utensils, which set upon the stove. These
were composed of a great pot, teakettle, and
bakepan. The fire burned briskly, the teakettle
hummed merrily, and I sat before the stove, my
face buried in my hands, gazing upon the live coals,
which shone out through a crack in the front part
of the stove. My thoughts were of the new position, and what was to become of it. Already I
beheld myself, after the manner of my male rela-
tives, promoted, one grade after another, until I
stood upon the deck of a noble fisherman, as her
commander. The moment I did that, the boat gave
a sudden lurch, which upset me, and down came
the great pot, full of boiling, hissing beans, upon
the cabin floor!

All know the story of the man who purchased
the glass ware, which he heaped before him, and sat .
contemplating its beauties, and the profits he was
to realize from its sale, until he had become a
princely merchant, and demanded the hand of the
Grand Vizier's daughter in marriage. It was refused. He kicked, and down crashed the glass
ware, and all his future prospects. Such, I felt,
was my position, as with a huge wooden spoon I
scooped up the beans from the cabin floor, keeping
an eye to windward, lest some of the mischievous
crew should come below and witness my mortifica-

tion. Despite this mishap, the first dinner on
board was a success. The beans went back into
the pot, and thence into the stomachs of the fisher-
men, for which they were originally intended.
The tars smacked their lips, praised the beans, the
cook, and complimented the cleanliness of the cabin
floor, which I had taken the precaution to wash.

I felt gratified at their praises, and my spirits
began to rise, as, after dinner, dish after dish was
placed by me upon the shelf, clean and shining.
The whole work was completed. I inwardly
chuckled at my success, and with the pan full of
dishwater mounted the gangway to go on deck
and "chuck" the contents overboard. Elation
added an extra force to my arm. The dishwater
went overboard and so did a dozen knives and
forks, which lay in the bottom of the pan, and
had escaped my observation. When I saw them
disappear beneath the waves, I felt a strong in-
clination to follow them. I was reserved however
for other mortifications. During the rest of the
voyage we operated at meal-time with wooden
utensils, whittled out for the occasion, which an-
swered for knives and forks. As the ship's larder was not overburdened with meats, we were
not troubled to any great degree.

Fishing occupied my attention for three years,

sometimes at the banks, and sometimes chasing
mackerel schools up and down the coast.

At the age of twenty I was in the boot and shoe
business, on Hanover street, Boston, being the jun-
ior member of the firm of Mansfield & Kemp, and
had made sufficient money, I thought, to take to myself a wife, who is the lady so often seen in a venerable cap and dress, occupying quite a prominent
position in the Old Folks' Concerts.

Soon after this I purchased a farm in Reading,
determined to enjoy the comforts of rural life, in
connection with my city business. I was at this
time attacked with a disease which has prevailed
to a great extent among my neighbors and friends
since my remembrance — " Fancy Farming." I
grew poor (in pocket) while the fever raged,
but was rich in experience after the patient was
cured. The malady included everything which
follows the purchase of land by a young man
who has enough to do without spending his time
among the hoes and rakes. One phase was the
" hen fever," and I never shall forget the feelings
of pride with which I contemplated that flock of
chickens, one hundred strong, that fed from my
hand one morning before I left for the city. But
in their tender years, just before the pin-feathers
had disappeared, a cold and violent storm came
in the night and with it came that terror of the

hen-roost, — a skunk. Between the two they made a "good haul." In the morning five forlorn and shivering chicks alone remained to tell the tale of that night of horrors. I concluded from this disaster that raising fowls was profitable only in those places not infested by unfavorable natural elements, and animals whose appetites are not commensurate with their bump of destructiveness.

I was very lucky in raising fruit. My trees were loaded with plump and luscious apples, the profits on which bid fair to heal the wounds to my pride made by the storm and skunk. A man was employed to pick and carefully pack them in barrels, and they were disposed of to Mr. Curtis of Faneuil Hall Market, the total yield being two hundred and twenty five barrels. After all expenses had been met, I counted my profits and found them to be exactly eight cents a barrel. That is the most lucrative agricultural operation I was ever engaged in.

A fine field of potatoes near the house was my especial pride, one year. The "rot" did for them what other things had done for the chickens. One morning I left two hundred hills of squashes in my garden; the hot sun beat down upon them, the bugs got lively and voracious, and when I returned at night they were wilted and broken.

A good portion of my time was passed in killing

caterpillars. It is a pastime edifying to the fancy
farmer, for only about one season. A rustic wants
variety as well as other persons. If the vermin
would change their nature, so that the brain might
be exercised to invent some new method of destruc-
tion, the slaughter might then be contemplated with
a certain degree of interest and pleasure; but a
caterpillar is the same worm as the seasons come
round, and there is but one way of killing him. He
is numerous, and requires incessant watching.

Winter came, and with it the long evenings, when
the people in the country, and especially the good
people of Reading, depend upon social intercourse
for their enjoyment. Like them I loved to be
cheered by the company of acquaintances and friends.
After a few evenings passed in quiet, and mostly in
bed, a thought struck me, from which has originated
the "Old Folks' Concerts," which have since become
so famous. There were many good singers in Reading, which also abounds in good things generally.
It is a model New England town, where the inhabitants are social, intelligent, and hospitable, and after
traversing so many thousand miles of my own and
foreign countries I have become convinced that *the*
fortunate day of my life was when I purchased my
farm of twelve acres in that suburb. But I digress.
One evening I invited a few young people (singers)
to my residence, to pass an evening in repeating

some of the popular songs of the day, with which we were all familiar. The first experiment was so successful that many evenings were passed in like manner. The voices blended well together, and, more than all, the good sentiment and pleasant associations made all feel that the time was well spent.

It then occurred to me to revive old memories by singing some of the tunes which strengthened the religious faith of our grandfathers and grandmothers, and had often been the medium through which our sturdy and pious ancestors had lifted their hearts in thankfulness to their Maker, for planting their home in the land of liberty. Accordingly the "country round about" was thoroughly scoured, and every old singing-book which could be procured was brought to my house on the next evening of the "sing." An odd collection they were, many of them being entire strangers to the present generation. Prominent among them was the noted Billings and Holden Collection, the others being made up of singing-books of more modern date, which contained old tunes. By paging the principal pieces in the different books, we soon had them readily at our command. These rehearsals attracted much attention in the neighborhood, and, on the evenings set apart for them, the house was crowded with those

2

who came to listen to the performances of the " Old Folks," as our neighbors familiarly called us.

Before proceeding with the account of the concerts it may be of interest to the reader to learn a few facts concerning the history of church music in New England.

CHAPTER II.

IN the early Puritan churches of New England but one psalm was sung in the morning, and this was dictated line by line to the congregation. One of the officers of the church usually read the hymns and gave out the tunes. In some parishes other persons performed this duty, — for which service the party was excused from paying his poll-tax. In the afternoon, "if there was time," a psalm was sung, and the services were concluded with a prayer and blessing. The first book printed in America was the "Bay Psalm Book," which was compiled, in 1640, by an association of New England Ministers. Its introduction met with great opposition, as the oldest of the Puritans in America were attached to Ainsworth's version of the Psalms, which they brought with them. The Salem churches used Ainsworth's work until 1667, and the Plymouth Church until 1692. The Puritan churches of the colonies were much divided in sentiment

upon questions incident to the subject of music in
the sanctuary. The records of the times show that
the colonists were much "exercised in their con-
sciences" in regard to whether the singing of the
Psalms of David with a lively voice was proper
under the New Testament dispensation. Whether
women as well as men, or men alone, should sing;
whether the "pagans" (the unconverted) should
be allowed to sing with the church members.
Many thought the old familiar tunes were inspired,
and were therefore opposed to the introduction of
any new music. Some individuals had scruples
about singing in a metre devised by man, and
others were puzzled with the question whether it
was lawful to read the psalm to be sung in public
worship. The above questions were considered
and discussed by the learned divines of the period.

For sixty years after many of the earliest churches
were gathered in New England not more than ten
tunes were used. These were written in the psalm-
book or the Bible, and were often repeated once or
twice in the services of a single Sabbath. In most
cases the psalms were sung in rotation without regard to the subject of the discourse. After a time
music had been so neglected that no congregation
could sing more than five or six tunes. These were
Oxford, York, Litchfield, Windsor, St. David's, and
Martyr's. In cases where the metre did not suit the

tune, one or two words were omitted to meet the difficulty. During the disputes and contentions of the Puritan churches, the cultivation of music was neglected, the use of notes fell into disrepute, and no two of the singers kept time together. In the quaint language of a writer of the times, — Rev. Mr. Walter of Roxbury, — " Every melody was tortured and twisted as every unskilful throat saw fit." The singing sounded " like five hundred different tunes roared out at the same time," producing noises " so hideous and disorderly as is bad beyond expression."

About the year 1700 a reform in church music was begun in Massachusetts, which made slow progress for a time, but an improvement was effected, however, without great opposition in many quarters, The attempts made to reform and improve the music in Puritan churches produced great excitement. Some parishes were divided into parties upon the question of singing by "note," or by "rote," and in many towns the parties were so equally divided upon the question that a compromise was made, and half the psalms were sung in the old and half in the new way. According to all accounts, the best singing in Massachusetts Colony for a hundred years after its settlement was in the Indian churches. Mr. Eliot translated the psalms into Indian verse. Copies of this work are extant, but

not a human being can read them. The Indian
church music is described as being excellent*— "singing of psalms with most ravishing melody."
Frequent mention is made by Puritan writers of the
" excellent singing of Massachusetts Indians."

To show the spirit of the times of which I speak,
I will quote from a writer in Massachusetts a hundred and fifty years ago : "Truly," said he, " I have
a great jealousy that if we once begin to sing by
note the next thing will be to pray by *rule* and
preach by *rule*, and then comes Popery !"

For many years after the arrival of the Puritans,
they cultivated music, but during the contentions
and bitterness of party strife upon religious matters, which soon so extensively prevailed, and the
witchcraft delusion, the Indian wars, and other evils
and troubles of the period, but little attention was
paid to harmony of any kind. About the year
1700 the clergy began to see with what difficulty —
and as one of them expresses it, " what great inde-
cency," — the singing was executed. Some of them
thought that singing would have to be wholly omitted in public worship, if the art was not revived.

The pulpit earnestly called for a better performance of their songs of praise, and the ablest
divines in the colonies joined heart and hand in the
reformation. It is at once instructive and amusing
to note what opposition the efforts for a musical re-

form encountered. In every parish the reform was opposed with a virulence of feeling and tenacity of attachment to old customs that seem to us at this day almost unaccountable. It may be affirmed that the witchcraft delusion met with less opposition at its introduction than was brought to bear against the singing reform. The deacons wished to retain their office of deaconing off the psalms, and opposed singing by note. For the curiosity of the reader I will give some of the reasons urged by the musical hawkers of a century and a third ago. These ultra conservatives opposed singing by note, because, "it was a new way, not so melodious as the existing custom." They opposed the innovation because there were so many tunes no one could ever learn them; they affirmed that the tunes were Popish in their tendency, and would lead to the *introduction* of *musical instruments!* They reasoned that

> "If gowns and cassocks are but rags
> Of Bab'lon's Scarlet Doxy,
> What is an organ piping psalms
> But worshipping —— by Proxy?"

But the pulpit stood firm amidst the popular clamors. Such men as the Mathers, Edwardses, Stoddards, Symeses, Dwights, Wises, Walters, Thachers, and Princes, fearlessly called for a musical reform. Many of the discourses of these divines are able arguments on the "Reasonableness of Regular Singing."

Rev. John Tufts, of Newbury, published a musical work, in 1712, entitled, "A very plain and easy introduction to the art of singing psalm tunes, with the cantus or trebles of twenty-eight psalm tunes contrived in such a manner as that the learner may attain the skill of singing them with the greatest ease and speed imaginable. Price sixpence, or five shillings per dozen." The work ran through eleven editions, and the number of tunes was increased to thirty-seven, all but one in common metre. The number of tunes in these little books was considered enormous. The pages were neatly engraved, and in size to bind with the "Bay Psalm Book." The reform went on steadily, and other musical publications soon appeared. Cotton Mather published a work in 1718, and Rev. Thomas Walter, of Roxbury, edited a work in 1721, which was the first music printed *with bass* in America. The work of Mr. Walter was recommended by pastors of the congregational churches, in Boston, except Cotton Mather, who had a rival work in the market.

Until about the year 1770, no native American had attempted to compose and publish a single tune. William Billings, a native of Boston, can claim the distinction of being the pioneer in this work.

Among the New England Puritans, singing

psalm tunes was always regarded as a devotional act. So great was the reverence in which the few tunes known was held, that the colonists put off their hats, as they would in prayer, whenever they heard one sung, as the English now do when "God save the Queen" is sung. The tunes which the "Old Folks" have given were held too sacred to be used for amusement.

Many of my readers of the elder generation will remember the excitement occasioned by the introduction of musical instruments into the churches of New England. Many parishes were divided and some were actually split by the innovation. It was wittingly said, "that the introduction of the violoncello and double bass was a base violation of the proprieties of God's House." Meeting-houses in which instruments were used or rejected were known as "Cat-gut," or "Anti-cat-gut churches." Even in our own day, the opposition to musical instruments in the sanctuary prevailed at the South and West. When the National Methodist Conference met in Boston, and the delegates from the different sections of the Union were invited by Honorable Benjamin Seaver, — then mayor of the city, — to Faneuil Hall, to be addressed by Daniel Webster, one of the clergymen, after attending public worship in the Hanover Street Methodist Church, wrote

home to a Southern denominational journal, that
there was no religion among the Methodists of Boston, for they had doors to their pews and organs in
their churches.

CHAPTER III.

AFTER the "dress rehearsals," I determined to appear in public, with my troupe, of whom I had began to feel somewhat proud. I saw that the entertainments pleased the "old folks," who did not belong to the choir. I felt also that a revival of the good music of former times, sung as our ancestors sung it, would be a novel experience to the present generation. Accordingly the evening of Dec. 6, 185– was set apart as the proper time for Father Kemp and his "Old Folks" to make their debut before the public. Extra pains were taken to procure books, and we found it difficult to get a sufficient number. Doubtless more old garrets in Massachusetts were turned topsy-turvy for this purpose than for any object since the settlement of the colony. At the first entertainment the Lyceum Hall in Reading was literally packed with what Mr. Jenkins would call a "large and fashionable audience," although a very

27

important number of the people present were noted
for the scrupulous care which they took to discard
everything of a fashionable nature. The timid
ones feared a "break down;" but not such an one
as our parents were wont to indulge in, in their
moments of hilarity. Hundreds remained outside
the building unable to gain admission, and listened
to the music of the "Old Folks;" and they thought,
with the audience, that the voices of the fossils
were remarkably fresh.

The people of Lynn had an awakening upon the
subject of old music, and the company, which by
this time had become quite well organized, received
a cordial invitation to appear in that place. We
started in teams for Lynn. A severe snow-storm
came on, which rendered it impossible for us to get
to the hall. As it has always been my principle
never to postpone a concert on account of the
weather, the Sagamore House was substituted for
the hall, and those who heard the performance
were anxious for a second trial, under more favor-
able auspices. We afterwards appeared in Lynn,
with marked success. In the morning after the
concert at the hotel we started for home. The
roads were drifted and it was intensely cold, the
thermometer being for the most of the day twenty de-
grees below zero. Several of the ladies were frost-
bitten. Shovels were procured to "clear the track,"

and thus we worked our passage back to Reading, where we arrived at 6 P. M. The distance from Lynn to Reading is ten miles. We were all day on the road. This was my first experience in going abroad to give concerts. Had I then forsaken the business, the facts in the case would have more than justified me in so doing.

The popular favor with which these unique entertainments had met, prompted me to consider the expediency of giving the citizens of Boston an opportunity to hear them. There was a natural shyness on my part, which was shared by my associates, as to the propriety of the undertaking. Having done business in the city for many years, I of course had many acquaintances, who would be influenced by the measure of my success. If I failed in giving satisfaction, I might as well also fail in the shoe business, and hereafter confine my operations to Reading and Lynn, where I was appreciated. But no man, in my vocation, can be completely discouraged at one failure. The motto of my customers, in purchasing boots, is, "Try, try again," until they find a pair which fits them; and I encourage the axiom. Why should it not apply to the concerts as well? I determined it should. I considered the matter carefully, and the more I considered the better I thought of it. When I had fully concluded to make the trial, I was convinced that the

affair ought to assume the proportions of a demonstration, — a protest of the "Old Folks" against
being ignored by their posterity. It was my desire to bring to the eye and ear of the citizens of
the New England metropolis the customs of the
good people of former generations — of whose characteristics as well as dress and behavior we all had
read, but which none had been permitted to observe.
To accomplish this there must be extensive labor and
research, in which not one but scores of people
must engage, and to the ardor with which the young
"Old Folks" entered into the enterprise, in attending
to the details and preparing for the occasion, is
due the success of the first concert in Boston.

The Tremont Temple was secured, and I told the
company we would try *one;* and if that "took,"
we would try another. An extra train was char-
tered to run from Reading to Boston, and return after
the concert. The singers numbered about fifty
ladies and gentlemen. Our friends turned out in
round numbers, all dressed in the costume of "old
folks," and those who went to the city to sing and
sit on the platform were about two hundred. Such
a collection of "nondescripts" was never seen in
the Temple before. Arrived at the depot, we
found a large crowd awaiting our coming. Twelve
omnibuses conveyed us to the concert-room, which
was packed with an audience, in which curiosity

seemed to be the prevailing element. All the tickets were disposed of several hours before the time announced for the beginning of the entertainment; door-keepers had been knocked down, and the crowd held possession of the staircase and lobbies. The public were evidently aroused, and I felt somewhat aroused myself when I learned what had been going on.

As the members of the troupe and their friends slowly filed on to the platform before the immense audience the noise and disturbance ceased, and all were intently engaged in examining the queer, quaint, and curious costumes which covered the apparently venerable forms before them. One lady wore a dress brought to this country more than two hundred years ago, by Major Willard. His daughter, at her marriage, wore it, and three other ladies were afterwards joined in matrimony while wearing the same dress. The material was satin damask, very rich and brilliant. Other ladies wore dresses of antique fashion, none of which were less than fifty years old, and several were known to be upwards of two hundred years of age. Most of the gentlemen appeared in knee-breeches, buckles, and cocked hats; one had a coat which was worn by one of the first governors of Massachusetts; a hat worn at the battle of Bunker Hill by Lieut. Parker, of Reading, covered the head of another, and the coats, cloaks, etc., were generally venerable, but well preserved. Everything that could not count up a hundred years was considered modern.

The people in the vicinity of Reading were very kind in making presents of old relics, which were highly valued by us. In the way of bonnets, I believe this first concert at the Temple displayed more material on fewer heads than had ever been seen in the building before. One of my champion bonnets would make a score of modern "Fanchons," "Lamballes," and "Marie Antoinettes." One of these formerly belonged to a lady in Salem, and has been introduced at all my concerts. When it was first purchased, all the young ladies in the neighborhood sat in judgment upon it, and decided that the owner must carry it "right straight back," as it was too small for the fashion! She kept it however, in hopes that the fashions might change. This bonnet was as large as a flour-barrel!

Among the distinguished persons represented by the troupe were George and Martha Washington, John Hancock, General Putnam, Thomas Jefferson, Daniel Boone, and numerous others equally well known, besides Puritan fathers and mothers. A member of the company appeared in a check worn by one of the Salem witches. The audience were much interested and amused, and evidently awaited the opening chorus with great eagerness. The selections comprised a variety of sacred and secular music, the latter being of more modern composition. The orchestra was no mean affair, the most notable object being the big fiddle, of whose venerable owner we shall speak hereafter. "Auld Lang Syne" seemed to put the immense throng in the right humor to enjoy the concert. The "Anthem for Easter," "Greenwich," "Coronation," "Strike the Cymbal," the "Ode on Science," etc., followed in due time, all being received with applause. The concert closed with the singing of "Old Hundred," in which the audience were invited to join. They complied with the request with a hearty good will. Notice was given that the "Old Folks" would soon appear in another concert at the Temple. They did appear, and eleven were given in succession with the same éclat that attended the first performance. As an instance of the interest excited among the elder people to hear the company, I will mention a gentleman from Brookline, who, after being disappointed in gaining admission to the Temple on three different evenings, got indignant and entered a complaint at my store, that he had come to the city with his family in a carriage on these occasions, and had found the doors closed and the house full each evening. "Now," said he, with righteous indignation flashing from beneath his spectacles, "I am more than seventy years old, but I could manage these

3

concerts better myself!" I took care of him and
his family after that, notwithstanding the fact that
half the tickets he had purchased were spurious.
The following is one of the many very kind notices
of this entertainment which appeared in the Boston
papers, and to whose influence I attribute much of
the fame which the "Old Folks" speedily acquired, —

"Half an hour before the performances of 'Father
Kemp's Old Folks' were commenced last night,
every inch of room within the Tremont Temple hall
was occupied, and hundreds came afterwards. The
excellence of this company was attested by this
great desire to hear them, and we feel some local
pride in chronicling this success, for they merit all
the patronage bestowed upon them; they are capable singers, perform good music, and all of their
actions are decorous and appropriate."

CHAPTER IV.

THE fame of the "Old Folks' Concerts" had now spread throughout New England. Invitations poured in from all quarters for the troupe to appear in not only the cities of this Commonwealth, but in those of the other States. Many of these were accepted, the first being given in those places to which access was easy, and from which the members of the company could return home either on the same evening or the next day. The system of making a liberal display of old folks on the platform was still kept up, — the expenses of those who would go in "full dress" for the occasion being borne by me. These first concerts were given for pleasure, and no thought of benefiting myself pecuniarily by them had been entertained. The bills, as presented to the manager, were very large, and the liberal patronage

alone enabled him to meet them. I did not depend
entirely upon the newspapers and board fences for
advertising. In addition to those powerful agents,
it was my custom to marshal the company, which
generally numbered from one to two hundred, and
parade them about the streets, to let the people
know how venerable and respectable we were. Of
course the members were particularly careful about
their toilets on these occasions, as they were frequently subjected to uncomfortably close inspection.
The children always followed us in the greatest glee,
the dogs barked, business was suspended, and old
men hobbled along beside us, with the light of other
days shining in their eyes. Young and middle-
aged people smiled or laughed, and the whole
neighborhood, wherever we appeared, was in an uproar, — just as we intended it should be. We were
amply repaid for these excursions by the looks of
curiosity and astonishment and the odd remarks
with which we were greeted. Our concerts in the
vicinity of Boston were much more enjoyable than
many others we have given. The experience was
novel and exciting to us, and the singers were
accompanied by a crowd of friends who shared the
merriment of every ludicrous incident, and when
there was a prospect that none would occur to
enliven us, the inventive faculties of some of our

own number would be exercised to set the company in a roar.

I was soon prevailed upon by offers from the West and South to visit the large cities in those sections. My agent was a young collegian, whose education and intelligence prepared the influential people whom he met, as he travelled before us, to give us a kind reception. The first route marked out was from Reading to Washington, — to stop and give concerts at each prominent place on the road. The company numbered forty-seven singers, — the ornamental portion who had previously figured in our entertainments being, of course, left behind.

When we appeared in Providence, Howard Hall was packed to its fullest extent. The company passed on to the stage and opened with " Auld Lang Syne," which was followed by the " Easter Anthem." The tune had scarcely been finished, when a venerable, white-haired gentleman, in the middle of the audience, tossed his hat in the air and shouted, " I knew it ! I knew it ! Every word of it ! " Of course the attention of the whole house was directed to him ; but he could not be pacified. He talked loudly of the old times, which the old costumes and old tunes had brought vividly before him. Amusing as the incident might seem, there were more tears shed than smiles provoked by it. He

became so much excited, that his son was compelled
to remove him, almost by force, from the audience.
I believe there was not a person present who would
not have gladly gone away if the old man could
have remained.

I have often stood upon the platform, while con-
ducting the choir, and watched the effect of some
of the stirring old anthems upon the audience.
While the young people would laugh and whisper
together as if criticising our odd costumes, the tears
were trickling down the furrowed cheeks of those
who were living over again their moments of youthful enjoyment.

After the first concert in New Haven, Mr. Daniel
Foss, who operated the "big fiddle," was the hero
of an adventure, which, at the time, occasioned
much merriment among the troupe. On returning
to the hotel, a lady of some note, who lived there at
the time, inquired of Mrs. Kemp, "where that old
man was who played the big fiddle?" She "desired
to see him, as she had something for him." Mr.
Foss was introduced in his every-day garments.
The contrast was so great that the lady said, "He is
not the gentleman. I want to see that *old* man."
Mrs. Kemp assured her that the "old man" stood
in her presence. She was still incredulous, and evidently begun to regard such "deception" upon a
lady of her standing, as an imposition. Other mem-

hers of the troupe came forward and agreed with Mrs. Kemp's statements. Still being in doubt, she invited him to her apartments and presented him with an elegant basket of fruit and wines, which he gracefully accepted, and returned the next morning in costume to thank her for the present. Mr. Foss is, to this day, reluctantly compelled to admit, that, had he fiddled without the aid of artistic embellishment to his person, he and his friends would never have enjoyed that splendid repast.

We left New Haven quite early on the morning after our last concert, in order to arrive in New York and do a little advertising before nightfall. The first concert was to be given at the Broadway Tabernacle. Our agent had procured a dozen fine teams, the horses being gayly decked with plumes. Of course we could not expect to "take" Gotham in any way except by "assault." So in full uniform, conspicuously seated in the carriages, we rode about the streets, and at once became the "observed of all observers." The urchins numbered, I should think, several millions, and their demonstration of welcome in the shape of snowballs, etc., was one which could alone be made by the juveniles of a great city. They followed us to the hotel, and filled the space in front, while we were alighting from the vehicles. A friend suggested that at the concert we should have to employ many policemen; but I

assured him this whole crowd would not be there.
So it proved. New York is a very large place, and
is generally supposed to admire the new rather than
the old. But the Gothamites did not slight the "Old
Folks." At the first entertainment the Broadway
Tabernacle was packed, and the enthusiasm among
the descendants of the Knickerbockers for the performances of the sons and daughters of the Puritans was even more marked than I had anticipated.

While in New York the company was invited to
attend one of Thalberg's concerts, which he gave
before the public schools. He was then at the
height of his success in America. There was something of a contrast between the efforts of the eminent and accomplished pianist and the homely,
straightforward performances of the "Old Folks;"
but I am inclined to believe that the children would
have voted *en masse* for Father Kemp, had they been
asked to signify their choice of the two portions of
the entertainment.

I was afterwards waited on by the Board of Education, who desired the "Old Folks" to attend one
of the noon concerts given before the children at
Niblo's Garden. I was never backward in seizing
upon an opportunity to appear in public where the
juveniles were assembled, for they rank among my
stanchest supporters. Many a parent has been induced to listen to our entertainments through the

marvellous stories of odd costumes, big bonnets and fiddles, and good music, narrated by the children of the public schools before which we sung. I at once accepted the invitation of the Board, impressed the importance of the occasion upon the company, purchased a full supply of white kid gloves, and, at the head of the troupe, in full costume, the "big fiddle" forming a sort of shield to the "Old Folks," marched along Broadway towards the Garden. When we arrived at the door, we met an obsta cle in the shape of some one interested in the establishment, who refused to permit us to enter the house. The member of the Board explained and expostulated, but the Teuton was inexorable, and declared that "Fader Kemps cannot enters dish deatre mit his old folks for an advertisement. De shildrens goes hum and says, 'Vat have we here like Fader Kemps and his company? Nodings, nodings.' So deir faders, deir mudders, deir kindreds all goes to see Fader Kemps and hear dem sing, and I can stay here mit my deatre all alone if I like. I understands his dittle game, and know sumdings about management. No, sir; Fader Kemps and his troupe goes into my deatre wen dey pays, — and not before. I vish you a very goot mornings."

I concluded the old fellow did know "sumdings about management," and beat a hasty retreat, fol-

lowed by my troupe. Such treatment may seem
unjust and uncharitable ; but I looked upon it as the
natural result of the schooling which my Dutch
friend had received. It is said that everything is
fair in love and war, and it should be added, theatrical management, also. Although I have no
reason to complain of bad treatment from theatre
managers, my experience as a "showman" convinced
me that in their business few advantages are given,
and many taken. But there is one thing which
should be mentioned to their honor. The members
of no profession are more ready to aid an unfortunate brother. Let his theatre be destroyed by fire ;
there is immediately a general "volunteering" of
lessees of other establishments, and of actors and
musicians, for a benefit. If a dull season depletes
his purse, no sooner is it known than his rivals are
proffering him generous assistance. Such humane
characteristics go far to redeem other less commend-
able traits. They have many difficulties to encounter, and many of those with whom they are
compelled to deal are a "sharp set." Is it any
wonder that they become sharp from habit and
association?

The incident above narrated "got into the papers,"
and greater attention was drawn to the "Old Folks"
than would have been had we sung in the theatre.

Had we made a second application, we might perhaps have been graciously received.

While in New York we gave a concert in the Academy of Music, which was attended by upwards of six thousand persons. The proceeds were devoted to a charitable object. In bidding farewell, to resume my tour South, I had every reason to feel highly gratified with the first series of concerts in the Empire City.

CHAPTER V.

ILLIAMSBURG was the first town taken after New York, and we captured it just as the children were leaving the public schools. A crowded audience greeted us there. At Brooklyn, Henry Ward Beecher's church was secured; and, previous to the concert, we took a couple of hours to examine the city, in full costume; and the inhabitants took occasion to examine the new-comers, who appeared in such old garbs. We gave several concerts in the vicinity, and left for Philadelphia.

The City of Brotherly Love gave us a characteristic welcome. The Quakers turned out in goodly numbers, and crowded Dr. Jaynes's new hall, then the largest in the State of Pennsylvania. Another of the laughable incidents continually occurring happened here, the venerable old man with the " big fiddle" again being the hero. During intermission it was the custom of the members of the troupe to mingle with the audience, who were greatly interested in examining the costumes. Mr. Foss remained upon the platform, evidently guarding his instrument. A very aged lady approached him, and, without any ceremony, entered into conversation with him. She said she had been in General Washington's family, and could very well remember how they all looked. Mr. Foss joined with her in bringing up reminiscences of which he had heard, and with which she was familiar. Suddenly she asked, "Do you remember the Dark Day?" This was a "poser." After a little hesitation he observed that she could undoubtedly remember *that* occurrence much better than he could. "But can't you remember *anything* about it?" she asked; "I can remember it about as well as if it had been only yesterday." The ancient musician acknowledged that his memory was very treacherous, and he had no *distinct* recollection of the anomaly. "May I ask your age, sir?" "Forty-three." "Well, I should say as much!" exclaimed the old lady, quite tartly. "It is no longer a wonder that you don't remember that great dark day!"

From Philadelphia we went to Washington, where we gave several concerts. Our experience at the National Capitol was of a somewhat curious and

trying description. Congress was in session, and
every house was full. We dined at one table, or
rather sat around it until we were ashamed to sit
longer, and then went abroad and finished dinner on
a beefsteak. Our trunks were at another house ; we
slept at still another, and received friends who visited us on the sidewalk. Mr. Buchanan was then
President, and of course, we honored him with a
visit. Surrounding the " Old Public Functionary,"
we sang a patriotic air or two, with which he seemed
delighted. That did not, however, prevent him
from maintaining the position that States had not
the right to secede, but, if they did, force could not
be used to keep them in the Union.

On Sunday we sang at the religious services in the
New Representatives' Hall. The room was crowded, and the preacher evidently wondered how he
had become so suddenly popular. We sat in the
Reporters' Gallery, and he had not been informed
of our presence. When we "struck up" the " Anthem for Easter " he turned his head round with a
startled air, which would have been amusing had it
not been for the solemn character of the occasion.
That occurrence, and the presence of an unusually
large audience, completely nonplussed him, and his
sermon proved the folly of any one but a man peculiarly gifted, attempting to preach without notes.
The discourse consisted mainly of "brothers and

sisters," "friends," and "you, the unconverted;" and I really felt relieved when he sat down, and we prepared to sing the closing tune.

Accompanied by a numerous party, we visited the tomb of Washington, at Mount Vernon.

Standing around the vault, with uncovered heads, the "Old Folks" sang, —

"Why do we mourn departed friends?"

The associations that clustered around the spot made the scene a very impressive one, and will always be vividly remembered by those who were present on the occasion. Returning, we stopped at one of the forts on the Potomac, and sung some patriotic airs to the soldiers quartered there.

During our stay in Washington, we visited the heads of departments, in costume. The Secretary of State greeted us cordially, and we were urged to give him a specimen of our old New England vocalism. We did not wish to do anything foreign to propriety in such a place, and therefore complied with his request. The Secretary of the Treasury showed us great hospitality, and, without drawing upon his funds, we favored him with a few selections. The reader will understand that we were not over-anxious to sing in these "irregular places," and did not comply without much urging. We had all we wished to attend to between sunset and ten o'clock. At

the War Department both battle hymns and
tunes of a pacific nature were indulged in. The
Secretary smiled grimly during each performance,
but did not signify which he preferred. The Secretary of the Navy of course preferred nautical
songs; but as that department is generally behind
the times, we sung nothing more modern than "A
Life on the Ocean Wave," "On Jordan's Stormy
Banks," etc., which seemed to gratify him, as he
asked us to come again, knowing, of course, that
our engagements would prevent us from complying
with his request. At the Patent Office they inquired if they shouldn't "put us through" the establishment, so that imitations might be prevented.
We declined, but experience has since proved that
if the use of Father Kemp's name could have been
retained exclusively by the originator of the *nom de
plume* it would have "put money in his purse."
The only fault I have to find with Washington was,
as Artemus would say, its "muchness." An extra
pair of legs is wanted for every one who is to travel
there. We received many invitations from public
dignitaries and did not wish to refuse. Consequently, during a week's visit, we were constantly on the
move, and when the order to "pack" was issued, the
members of the troupe obeyed with more than their
usual alacrity.

Leaving Washington, we gave concerts in Baltimore, Philadelphia, and other cities on our way home. Hundreds of incidents of this homeward trip might be mentioned, but the reader can by this time imagine the ludicrous character of some of them. The press everywhere received us with the greatest favor, and to the editorial fraternity I was, in this first tour, indebted for many kind words which were not expected, and which aided materially in the success of the enterprise. As an instance of the manner in which we were "noticed," the following from an Albany newspaper is published,—

"An immense audience gathered in Albany Hall to *see* the 'Old Folks' and listen to the concert; and, altogether, it was about as satisfactory an exhibition and entertainment as has been enjoyed by our people for a long time. They came, they said, to show the costumes worn, and sing the hymns sung by their fathers and grandfathers, mothers and grandmothers, in the good old days; both of which they did. The costumes, we doubt not, were as they said, some of them actually handed down from a hundred or two years past, and others exact transcripts of the earlier fashions. By their consideration in passing through the aisles among the audience, a near view of their quaint costumes was had, which, we doubt not, occasioned much astonishment in the crowd at the want of good taste in the earlier days in the matter of dress. Half a century

hence, however, when present fashions get old, and
comparisons are in order, it may be a question
which age exhibited the most taste. The oyster-
shell bonnet may be looked upon as liable to the
same objections of taste as the dredge-bucket
bonnet of earlier days now is.

"The hymns, such as were and are yet popular in
church choirs, were given with great spirit and
effect; considerably more, we apprehend, aided by
the fine instrumentation, than our forefathers were
in the habit of rendering them. To see such profane innovations as the fiddle, the flute, the horn,
the trombone, introduced into a concert of sacred
music, which we were asked to imagine was being
given by our great grandmothers and grandfathers,
was a terrible assault upon the imagination, which
nothing but the excellent effect of these profane
additions could reconcile us to. We thought if our
fathers did not have or did not tolerate such aids to
their worship, they ought to have done so, and we
permitted the imagination to conceive that having
revisited the pale glimpses of gas-light to revel in
the melodies of olden times, they had brought back
with them a better judgment in connection with
their excellent melodies. The devil has had the
best music and the best instruments for a long time;
and, if our church-leaders of modern days would
gather a hint from the effect of this instrumentation

in making church music popular, they might turn the most effective weapons of Satan against him, and make a large stride towards the overthrow of his kingdom. Seldom, we apprehend, have our people had an opportunity of hearing this church music rendered with such inspiring effect and such an elevating influence; and if all those in the immense crowd who could sing had accepted the invitation of the leader, and joined in 'Coronation' and 'Old Hundred,' it would have been a 'sing' which would have been remembered for many a day, and with good effect."

The following, from a Rochester journal, will indicate the character of our audiences, —

"Father Kemp, with his accomplished band of singers, gave another of his peculiar and highly pleasing entertainments on Saturday evening, — one of the most attractive we have ever listened to. The audience was made up largely of the *élite* of the city; clergymen, physicians, lawyers, merchants, besides a goodly number of the more indispensable and therefore *better* class, — the *common people;* all, apparently, electrified, from the commencement to the close, with the novel appearance of the troupe, and their harmonious chords in the singing of the ancient songs and anthems which were so popular in the times of our great grandfathers."

CHAPTER VI.

FTER the completion of the first tour, I passed the summer quietly in Reading. When the hot weather was over, I made preparations to visit the great West and give concerts with the troupe of "Old Folks." I had received many cordial invitations from that quarter, and all assured me of a warm welcome. I was fortunate at this time in securing the services, as agent, of Mr. Henry C. Jarrett, a gentleman who has since become widely known as one of the most sagacious and enterprising theatrical managers in the country. He possesses rare abilities for organization, and proved, in my experience with him, the "right man in the right place." I am indebted to his trials and sufferings, in arranging the details for our appearance at various places, for many moments of comparative ease and quiet. His zeal and ingenuity knew no bounds; and he could generally see a clear sky ahead, whether we were stuck in the mud or blinded by darkness.

We left home on the 20th of September, with the intention of giving concerts in the principal cities and towns on our way. The tour lasted seven months, and during the whole period a concert was given *every evening*, Sundays excepted. Frequently we gave two concerts on the same night, — one to begin at $6\frac{1}{2}$, and close at $8\frac{1}{2}$ o'clock; and the other to begin at 9, and close at $10\frac{1}{2}$. This was done only in those places where the halls were too small to accommodate all who desired to attend them. The company on these occasions were, as a general rule, not sorry when "Old Hundred" was given for the second and last time. Mr. Jarrett would also frequently arrange for a mid-day concert, where the distance between the principal towns was not too long to prevent. By stopping over one train we could give a concert and general satisfaction to large audiences in some country village, take the next train, and arrive at our destination in time to appear in the evening. This vigorous management kept us well in harness, our voices and instruments in tune, and prevented our pockets from being depleted.

In Cincinnati we sang in ten concerts, and then took the company to Louisville, having engaged passage on the splendid steamer " Jacob Strader."

I made a bargain with the agent of the boat to stop
at Madison, on the way down, long enough to give
a concert. We left Cincinnati on a beautiful morning. Thousands of people covered the banks of
the river, while the windows of the houses in the
vicinity were crowded with ladies, waving handkerchiefs, and making other demonstrations of sorrow
or gladness (I never was fully convinced which) at
our departure. As the steamer moved away from
the wharf, we sang "Sweet Home," and several
patriotic airs, which were loudly cheered. We
arrived at Madison at 8 P. M., amid the roaring of
cannon and a grand display of fireworks, with
which the citizens had chosen to welcome us, as if
we were a company of brigadier-generals, fresh
from some gory field. The hall at Madison was
packed, much to the disappointment of the hundreds who came with us on the steamer, under
promise of a free pass to the entertainment. They
got their free passes, but certainly it was not my
fault if they could not get into the hall. I could
not stop to sympathize with them, as the audience
were impatiently awaiting our appearance.

After the concert the steamer conveyed us to
Louisville, arriving there early the next morning.
In that city we remained a week, giving eight concerts, and then started for Evansville, Ind., where
we appeared in entertainments with considerable

success. Our experiences in Indiana were of a very peculiar and trying nature; and our sojourn among the Hoosiers revealed traits in petty officials which it is hoped have, by the present time, been obliterated by the migration of civilized beings to those parts. Provisions had not been made for our accommodation at the hotel in Evansville; and, when the steamer landed us, the landlord had but one room, which he said was rather small for forty persons. So it proved, but to the best of my recollection, we did as well as we could under the circumstances. In the morning after my arrival I was told that licenses for my entertainments must be purchased. I procured them, — one from the State and one from the town. When the concert had begun, I was called out, and the performance was suspended for some time. The people on the stage wondered, and the audience wondered what the trouble was; and so did I, until a person whom darkness prevented me from recognizing informed me I must pay a license for Agriculture!

"I don't know who Mr. Agriculture is," I replied, "and I cannot satisfy his demand. I have already purchased two licenses."

"That don't make no odds, mister, you can give me five dollars or go to jail. I've got the officer here to take you if you resist."

I was too indignant to pay the five dollars, and

too far from home to go to jail; but the audience
were getting impatient and uproarious, and there
was no choice. So I gave him the money, with the
determination that "Agriculture" should some day
pay it back to me. But I must confess, "Agriculture" always got the best of me.

This is but one of scores of similar incidents that
happened in this section which could be mentioned
if space allowed.

If any one who reads this has ever experienced
the effects of a rain-storm in Indiana, he will know
how to sympathize with me when I inform him that
I have been through one and been compelled to meet
and overcome its attendant horrors. The mud
reigned supreme, and swallowed up almost everything but our determination to wade through it.
Our agent had secured by telegraph the old court-
house in one of the interior towns which we were to
visit. He had never seen it,— if he had, we should
surely not have been announced to appear there.
The people of the county must have been unusually
mild and respectable, as the sequel will prove. So
secure was the house of justice, that not even a
lock was placed upon the door. We arrived in
town about an hour previous to the time for beginning the concert, and when I saw the person who
had charge of the edifice, he informed me that "he

didn't hardly think the court-room would be 'zactly
fit for the reception of company that evenin'."

"Why so?" I asked, in amazement.

"Why *so?* Wal, I reckon you won't ask when I
tell you."

"Well?"

"You see, Neighbor Daggett, as lives in that yaller
house yonder, lost onc of his best keows durin' the
storm, 'bout a month ago; the river riz durin' that
storm amazingly, an' we begun to think we should
hev to git eout of these parts, and go onto the high
land afore long."

"But, my dear sir, what has that to do with the
court-house or the concert? You see it is almost
time for commencement."

"Wal, I wuz goin' to say, Deacon Daggett's
keows, they got kinder restless and broke down
the bars and all got eout of the pen. One was
found up here in a mud-slough almost drowndid,
and another strayed way down here to the heater
piece, and —"

"Confound the cows and the heater piece!"

"Be patient, stranger, be patient! The speckled
keow never come back; but the deacon is pretty
well to do, and he could afford to lose her; but he's
had a sort of mania on the subject since, and has
been tryin' to find eout what become of that keow.

'Twan't the wuth of the keow though, but the old
gentleman's curiosity."

"My dear friend, please omit details, and come
to the nub at once!"

"That's what I'm at. Wal, you see" (here he
changed his tobacco quid to the other side of his
mouth), "when I opened the door this morning,
there lay that speckled keow rite before the judge's
seat, on the floor. The poor critter must hev suffered, and had banged round considerable. You
see the storm was about a month ago, and it don't
smell very agreeable jest now. I don't think it's a
proper place to take ladies anyhow. I was goin' to
take my wife, but hev concluded I shan't. I reckon
the fellers won't mind it though. The door slammed
tew, evidently, and shet her in. Daggett allus said
that speckled keow was the most knowin' critter he
ever see; but it 'pears her knowledge was at last
the death of her."

I stopped to hear no more philosophical remarks.
I was satisfied I could not give a concert in the
court-house, and I went to work to do the best I
could. I despatched my aids as a general would at
the critical moment of a battle; and, in half an hour,
the bells of the village were ringing, and a crier was
shouting that "The Old Folks' Concert will be
given at the hotel instead of the court-house." The
room at the "tavern" was very small, about the size

to accommodate my company, and there were no seats; "standing room only," being the order of the evening. Nevertheless, the cash was taken at the outer door, and the entertainment paid pretty well — for us. I beat time with my baton, mounted on a flour barrel.

The next morning we were to leave town, but I was earnestly urged to give another concert before our departure. At last I consented. The court-house .was cleansed, the bells rung again, and the people were informed by crier that we should appear on that evening in the place lately occupied by the dead cow. Notwithstanding unpleasant remembrances, the house was crowded. When we were all ready to leave the next morning, up stepped one of the "license men," and demanded his fee, which I paid. Before we started, I was obliged to pay still another, and then I learned that more "officers" were looking for me, but I could not be found.

So much for the small towns of Indiana.

CHAPTER VII.

T is unnecessary for the reader to follow the "Old Folks" from place to place, in order to learn of what transpired during our visit to the Western States. I propose, in this chapter, to relate a few incidents which occurred while we were accomplishing the journey; and one of them I must mention before we get out of Indiana; for there, in the commonwealth noted for its alacrity in unmarrying people, I encountered more difficulties than in all the rest of the States combined. Indiana, as a State, is all right. Her sons did nobly in the war, and she has become one of the most noted sisters in the Union, on account of the industry, enterprise, and intelligence of her leading citizens; yet I cannot conscientiously recommend her as a fertile field for the showman, whether his intentions be benevolent or pecuniary. After I left Evansville I found that "Agriculture" still haunted me, and I discovered that he was one of the component parts of the State, of whom (or which) I should not be rid until I crossed her borders. In one of the "small towns" another occurrence transpired which both amused and vexed me. I always believed in "management," and when I told the mayor of "his native village" that I should be happy to extend the courtesies of the box-office to him, he winked knowingly, and said, "All right; never mind about the license,"—just what I thought he would say. "How many tickets would you like, sir?" "Wal, my family is not very large for these parts, — only twelve, — below the average; but they would all like to go and hear the 'Old Folks.'" "A small family, indeed, sir," I replied; "in Massachusetts we frequently count up twenty in one household." (I referred to hotels, of course.) "Why, you don't say so! Wal, I declare! I've allers hearn say that the Pilgrim Fathers were an industrious set; but, plague me, I didn't think they were so numerous up there! Hev some whiskey? It's new, but potent."

His eye rested upon a demijohn in the corner of his "office" (he was a carpenter by trade), which looked as if it had been used more frequently than any of the tools which were lying loosely about.

I excused myself from imbibing, and left the "City Hall" to make arrangements for the concert.

After the entertainment I received a note, which informed me that the Mayor desired to see me "across the way." I went "across the way," and found him in a beer saloon, where, I learned, he passed most of his time. He was a little "boozy;" and, when he arose to address me, he with difficulty steadied himself.

"Sir," said he, "as the Mayor of this village, I demand the five dollars' license required for Agriculture."

"Why, my dear sir, you said the license was all right, if I would pass your family."

"Sir! I cannot be bought! Pay, or go to jail! Your 'Old Folks' Concert' is a d—d humbug! Pay your license, or go to jail!"

"Come over to the hall, my friend, and I will settle with you."

He came over.

I then stated the facts of the case to my company, and asked them if they would go to jail with me. They all volunteered, with one voice.

"But, s-s-sir, our jail is not big enough to accommodate you all!" said he, as he tried to collect his wits; "I can take only the principal offenders."

"We must all go, or none," I replied, with difficulty restraining my risibilities.

"Kemp," said he, after trying to bring his eyes to bear steadily upon me, "Kemp, you are a good fellow and a Christian; your "Old Folks" sing pious tunes, and they should be rewarded for it; give me a dollar, and I will release you from arrest."

I gave him the dollar, and watched his retreating form until the door of the saloon again shut him from sight.

When we arrived in one of the towns of the West, where the German element predominated, I found that the hall where we were announced to appear contained no seats; there were no means of warming the room, no stage, and no facilities for lighting. Here was a "regular fix," indeed. I at once secured the Methodist Episcopal Church for my concert, and sent a big colored crier about the streets to announce the fact; but he did not speak a word so that it could be understood. However, the people learned that there was some unusual commotion, and began to inquire the cause. The result was, the church was filled; whereas the hall, had that been occupied, might not have been half full. When I requested the bill of the landlord of the "tavern," the next morning, I found that he made charges for thirty people, whereas my company consisted of but twenty-five.

"How is this?" I inquired. "Please subtract the bill of five persons from this, and I will pay it."

"Not if I knowsh mineself," said the old Dutch-

man, with imperturbable coolness, as he puffed
away at his meerschaum.

"Why not? I have only twenty-five people with
me."

"Look at your bills, Mishter Kemps. It hangs
up dare agin de walls. 'Fader Kemps and his
company of Old Folks, consisting of dthirty performers.' "

" Well, but thirty performers have not eaten your
corn bread and bacon."

"Dat makesh no dthifferensh mit us. Ve understands you, and hev been hombogged too moosh by
showmans. If you advertise dthirty you pays for
dthirty, venever you shtops mit me."

I was more amused than incenséd at the old
fellow's meanness. I had struck a new vein, and I
thought I could do no better than to pay for my
experience. So he receipted my bill for "dthirty "
people.

While travelling through Southern Illinois, which
is familiarly known as "Egypt," we stopped in one
town which bore such a hard reputation that we almost feared for our safety ; and, had it not been for
Mr. Jarrett's courage, we should surely have skipped
the place. It was a decidedly shy-looking town,
and I did not see an honest face in the whole audience. The vocalists executed the " tremulo " without much difficulty, and evidently regarded their

auditors as so many hungry wolves, ready to pounce upon them and capture their baggage. People at the East can scarcely imagine what a hard "Egyptian" town is. None of their laws or law officers are respected, reading and writing rank among the lost arts, and a church-goer is looked upon as a dangerous member of the community. We dared not remain in town over night, and had made arrangements to take the midnight train for another place nearer the borders of civilization. After the concert, we were travelling along the muddy road between the hall and the depot, enveloped in Egyptian darkness; many of the troupe doubtless expected an assault from a band of ruffians, and were keeping their eyes open for any emergency. I stepped upon a hoop, which flew up and struck me in the throat. I must confess I was startled, and think the word "garroter!" escaped my lips. This little incident brought the company at once to their senses, and they made the "welkin ring" with their merry laughter at my expense. I believe the whole troupe were heartily ashamed of the fears which they entertained of the inhabitants of that terrible town. I was determined to have no trouble there, and gave orders to take everything offered at the doors for admission fee, — bogus money, garden sauce, dried apples, or any other commodity. When the receipts

5

were examined, about fifty counterfeit half dollars
were among the favors bestowed upon us.

My experience with postage-stamps at the beginning of the war was a losing game with me. In
some places, nearly two hundred dollars'worth of
this adhesive currency would be taken. Most of
the stamps were enclosed in a small envelope, and
marked "25 cts." An examination frequently dis-
closed only one stamp, and that, in many cases, had
previously travelled hundreds of miles on a letter,
and been removed for the purpose of cheating old
people.

The cultivation of an even temper and a humane
disposition is absolutely necessary to the happiness
of a showman.   Sometimes instances occur where
expletives, and, perhaps, profane words, can alone
give relief.   " Swearing by rule " cannot be indulged
in by the experienced showman.   The occasions
which require the use of forcible language are so
numerous and unexpected, that," Darn it," "I vow,"
"I van," "Blast your picture," etc., even if used
sparingly, would soon become stale ; therefore I
adopted the rule to look charitably upon the short-
comings of those who ignored my rights to proper
respect and treatment, and never swore at them, but
passed on to the next town.   In all places, even
those where the enthusiasm for the "Old Folks" was
greatest, there were always persons who regarded

Father Kemp as a sort of public gold mine, which they had a perfect right to operate upon, and, if possible, exhaust. If these gentlemen have made anything out of the director of the "Old Folks' Concerts," his worst wish for them is that they will enjoy it as much as he did the sport of seeing them make it. So farewell, license officer, farewell old Dutch landlord, farewell, village mayor! Your world is a small one, but you unquestionably make more out of it than any other three men who enjoy the same privileges that you do.

CHAPTER VIII.

CANNOT follow further the history of the "Old Folks' Concerts," without mentioning a very worthy class whom I frequently met, and with whom I have passed many pleasant hours, — railroad conductors. A more genial, generous, and whole-souled set of men does not travel by steam. They have many obstacles to contend with, in the shape of Jeremy Diddlers of both sexes; bogus free passes ; bouncing boys and girls, reduced to half price ; importunities of nervous and hysterical females, who are afraid they will be left at the wrong station; large travelling companies, whose managers never pay unless compelled to ; and many other minor but not less irritating combinations. I have no fault to find with their treatment of the "Old Folks." Conductors with whom I have dealt will acknowledge that I always paid full fare for the troupe when their orders did not allow them to take half; and half-fare has been gladly given when arrangements, satisfactory to both parties, could not be made for my company to accept the hospitalities of the road. The latter compliment has always been courteously received by me, whenever offered, but I have not been over-burdened with invitations of that sort. That, however, is not the fault of the conductors.

One experience which I had is, perhaps, worth relating. During the seven months' western tour, while giving a concert in a large city, a tall, lank, overgrown young man, about nineteen years of age, presented himself at the door, representing himself as the son of Conductor ———, of the ——— Railroad, and desired to pass in upon that recommendation. His appearance was anything but prepossessing. He could not, however, prevent the six feet at nineteen, the long stride, round shoulders, drawling speech, and awkward locomotion. Appearances were against him; but he passed in. The troupe were to ride about a hundred miles with his father the next day. I saw no more of the youth, but kept his physiognomy in mind. The next morning we were seated in the cars, and moving rapidly towards our destination. The conductor entered, and accosted me with a gruff "Hollo! how many people have you got? Tickets, sir!" I looked at him. The son was a "chip of the old block!"

"Well," I replied, "I haven't exactly got the .
tickets; of course we can make some arrangement
for my two dozen of passengers?"

"Don't know about that, sir, — against the rules,
— must obey orders!"

"Suppose," said I, "you pass on and collect your
fares, and then return to me, when you will have
more leisure.. In the mean time I will count up."

"Very well; count up;" and he passed on.

My "counting up" consisted in cudgelling my
brain as to where I should strike the weak spot in
this imperious official. When he again passed
through the car I made the assault myself. As he
came by me I moved along in the seat, and said,
with "one of my most winning smiles," "Sit down,
my friend!" Of course he expected a settlement,
and that was what I wanted. But I begun in a
different way from what he anticipated. "I met a
son of yours last night, Mr. ———," I said, per-
suasively, and, I firmly believe, insinuatingly.

"Ah! which one? Abimelech or Ezekiel?"

"Abimelech, I think, — the tallest one." I ventured this much. I guessed at the name, and felt
it to be impossible for him to have a taller boy than
the one who visited my concert.

"Oh, yes; that was Abimelech. He spoke of
the concert, but said nothing about meeting you."

"He was probably carried away with the music;

but, if you should ask him, you would find that he knew Father Kemp."

"Well, I dare say."

"That boy," I remarked, "has many striking points in his personal appearance. His head is a noble one."

"Do you know, Mr. Kemp, that is what everybody says?" he asked, his whole countenance lighting up.

"Undoubtedly. Fathers, however, are apt to be blinded to the superiority of their children. That son of yours has a glorious future before him. I knew you at once, from his striking resemblance to his parent."

"Ah! Everybody says he looks like his father."

"He does indeed, — a father ought to be proud of such a son."

"And indeed I am."

"That boy ought never to have his quick and sensitive mind subjected to the drudgery of a commonplace calling, — a trade, or a position where muscle and not intellect is required."

"That is what I have been thinking of. What do you think he is best fitted for?"

"Science, the law, or medicine; or, if his disposition is of a devout nature, the ministry. I have met thousands of these professional men during my travels; I watch them; I note their cast of coun-

tenance, and require no one to inform me upon
their characteristics. I do not pretend to be a
Lavater; but there are some traits of character,
which are written indelibly in a man's face, and
experience has made them plain to me."

Two of my troupe were sitting behind me.

"What is the old coon driving at?" I heard one
ask.

"We shan't see the point till we get to our destination," replied his companion. "See if old daddy
draws his calfskin."

"Then you really think,"·resumed the conductor,
"that Abimelech has great gifts?"

"Unquestionably. They are stamped on his
massive brow, in his searching eye, firm mouth, and
in fact all over his finely shaped head. Has Pro-
fessor Fowler or any noted phrenologist ever
examined his bumps? As for myself I am a great
believer in phrenology. Had it not been for that
remarkable science I might have been at this time
walking the deck of a fisherman or keeping a shoe
store."

"I think there is something in it myself, and
have often been exercised about the matter. I will
have Abimelech's bumps examined."

Here the cars stopped at a way station, and the
conductor left me and attended to his duties. I
drew a long breath, looked at the table of distances,

and found that thirty of the hundred miles were completed! I almost dreaded his return, although by this time I felt sure of a "compromise."

He again appeared and voluntarily took his seat beside me. "That boy," said he, "is marvellously given to studying up things. In matters of history, such as the Revolution, the war of 1812, and the landing of the Pilgrims, he is a good deal better posted than I am."

"I don't doubt it. I presume he could give me information upon the history of my native State, — Massachusetts."

"Just as likely as not."

"Speaking of Massachusetts, reminds me that I have a home there in the immediate neighborhood of where the bloody battles occurred, which sounded the knell of British tyranny in America. If you ever visit that State, by all means bring that boy with you. Nothing could please me more than to *reciprocate your kindness* (this was greatly emphasized) by devoting a day or even a week to you. I would show you where the first shots were fired in State Street; I would follow the road where Paul Revere took his midnight ride to awaken the patriots that they might be prepared for the enemy; visit Lexington Common, and ascend with you to the top of Bunker Hill Monument, which looks down upon the spot where Warren fell — I would — "

Just as I said "fell" the cars again stopped, and the conductor darted out to attend to the passengers who were leaving and taking the train. He soon returned, and I continued my discourse in the same strain. "*I feel grateful for your courtesy*," said I, "and, independently of that, my interest in your son prompts me to offer you hospitalities which it is not my custom to present to a stranger."

"I calculate to come to Massachusetts next summer, and I think I shall take Abimelech with me."

"If you do, by all means visit Father Kemp at Reading. I shall be there leading a quiet life, with nothing to do except to treat my friends handsomely, and devote my time to their enjoyment."

Twenty miles more accomplished.

The stops during the last fifty miles were more frequent than they had been during the ride. His duties were therefore more varied. He often appeared to me, and, on each occasion, I either reminded him of his son's intellectual countenance, and how much he looked like his father, or spoke of the pleasant days we were to pass in visiting the scenes of the old Revolutionary fights.

Before we completed our journey, he had confidentially informed me upon many important points in his family history, and I had told him many things in my own experience, dwelling particularly upon the kindness and consideration shown me by conductors. I think he enjoyed that ride, for when the "Old Folks" alighted at the place of their destination, he had forgotten all about the fares. He grasped me warmly by the hand, and gave me a pump-handle shake, evidently regarding me as one who had done him a great favor. I pump-handled him in return, for I knew he had done me one. As the cars moved off, I stood upon the platform, my countenance, as I imagined, wreathed in smiles, waving a graceful adieu to the generous conductor. The last words I heard from him, as he caught the guard, and swung his long body upon the steps of the car were, "Abimelech and I will see you next summer."

I have no apology to make to the reader for the foregoing confession. No one but a showman can appreciate the embarrassing situation in which I was placed.

My experience with the schools was often a very curious one. In most of the places which I visited the rules in regard to permitting children to attend any kind of performance were very stringent, and I often found it difficult to get a hearing. On these occasions I set aside my native modesty, and let boldness do what ingenuity could not accomplish.

I have frequently taken a carriage to go the rounds
of the schools, when the fact would become known
to some committee man, and he would take another
and follow immediately after, with the intention to
stop my proceedings. My plan was generally to
enter unceremoniously, and excuse myself to the
teacher, tell her who I was, and ask if she would
like tickets to my entertainments. They were never
refused. I then began to talk to the children, while
she stood tremblingly by, and evidently desiring to
tell me that I was violating the rules of the committee. If one ventured to remind me of the fact,
she was confidentially informed that the committee
were "all right."

Once, in a rural district of Vermont, I encountered a formidable obstacle, which almost unfitted
me for the duties I was to perform. I entered the
school-room, and apologized by saying I supposed I
was to step into the entry. I held out my hand,
which the teacher did not grasp. I always shook hands
with school-mistresses, and have probably done more
in that line than any other man in the country. She
drew back, and blushingly said she had a bad humor,
and I might not like to shake hands with her. I assured her it would be a pleasure. But she still de-
murred. The urchins (about sixty of them) were
looking with eyes and mouths wide open upon this
unceremonious interruption of their studies and mis-

chief. Suddenly a little bright-eyed chub in the middle row called out, —

"Don't you do it, mister; the school-ma'am has got the itch!"

The effect of the warning can be better imagined than described. I think that youngster had to "take it" after I was gone. I should not have narrated this story, which is true in every particular, had I not lately seen, in many first-class newspapers, an advertisement headed "Itch! Itch! Itch! Scratch! Scratch! Scratch!" There is, therefore, no impropriety in it, according to the public press. Should this meet the eye of the above-named teacher, the fact that the papers look upon the disease as a public calamity may serve as a balm for her wounded feelings, and make her regret that she whipped the boy for speaking "out loud" in school.

CHAPTER IX.

WHEN I visited Philadelphia, it was estimated that there were about ninety-two thousand children attending the public schools. I called on a member of the Board of Education, and told him I wanted to do a favor to the younger generation, and therefore desired very much that they should all have an opportunity to see and hear the "Old Folks." To accomplish an object at once so benevolent and important, I had determined, after due deliberation, to reduce the price of admission to a concert, for the children, to fifteen cents. The cost of giving my performances was enormous; but, in making the sacrifice, I felt that I was doing a favor for which I should feel justified, even if my expenses should be greater than the receipts.

The member with whom I was dealing was a lawyer by profession. He listened to my "eloquent" address, and, after assuring me that he duly appreciated my self-sacrificing disposition, fixed his eye upon me with a knowing, quizzical look, and said, —

"My good Father Kemp, ninety-two thousand fifteen-cent pieces is a good deal of money."

I felt the force of his remark, and began to be afraid I should not see the money. But I argued the case with him, dwelling mainly upon the point that it would not be creditable in Philadelphia to form an exception to all the other cities of the Union which I had visited. Before we parted I believed I had made an impression, — a fact which was at last verified. For, before I left Philadelphia, the school children attended the concerts, and our treasury showed the receipt of *nearly* ninety-two thousand fifteen cents.

Attempts to secure proper halls in some of the rural districts were sometimes fruitless, and the efforts often gave rise to very amusing incidents. At a village in Connecticut, once, I called on the selectmen, and desired the use of the town hall. Two of them readily consented, but the third one, who felt great responsibility in the matter, could not "conscientiously" agree to the proposition. I explained to him my object in coming to the village, which was to give the natives a great treat,— to show them how our forefathers and mothers dressed, and sung the good old tunes. He looked solemn and wise,

but could not understand what kind of a performance was intended.

" We have a good town hall," said he, " and if it
is a *sarkis* that you have got, I cannot conscientiously consent to let you have it. I don't want any
horses in there ! "

I commiserated his clouded mental vision, and
stopped argument. After passing an hour with him,
in which time I detailed all the plans of the entertainment, he reluctantly gave his consent to the use of
the hall. I plastered over his "conscience" with
tickets for himself and family before he had consented to let the "good town hall."

While in Connecticut, it was my good fortune to
meet Abraham Lincoln, who was then on a lecturing
tour in that State. Of course I had at that time no
idea of his future elevation to the Presidency, and
my remembrance of him, as I remarked to a friend,
when I heard of his nomination, was that he was
" one of the most entertaining men I ever knew."
He had an anecdote to illustrate every point which
was brought up in conversation, and I passed, in the
cars and at the hotels, many pleasant hours in his
company. His lectures were political, and, of
course, attracted principally the male portion of the
inhabitants, and, as we frequently "performed" in
the same place, he jocosely proposed to "swap"
audiences once in a while, as he was tired of speak-

ing to so many heads not covered by bonnets. I was much impressed with his peculiar power, but did not then anticipate that he would develop qualities which would place him among the wisest statesmen and foremost humanitarians of the age.

In New Bedford, once, we remained over Sunday, and the "Old Folks" were invited to sing in the evening at the church of my friend, Rev. Mark Trafton, as a part of the service. The intention was not to have the fact become generally known; but it did; and such a crowd! The house was packed long before the time of commencement, and it is believed not a pew-owner got into the building. The audience was evidently composed mostly of those who had never been to church before. My choir sung one tune. When it was concluded, the "most enthusiastic applause," as the theatrical critics say, followed; the spectators (not worshippers) clapped hands and stamped feet, while the "peanut brigade" in the galleries whistled and hooted with double their usual zeal. The situation was painful and ridiculous. After a few vain attempts to calm the storm, the minister dismissed the congregation, and the "Old Folks" were ever afterwards found "at home" on Sunday evenings.

Not long before the occurrence above narrated, I had an experience with some Pennsylvania deacons, which reminded me of the early struggles to intro-

duce instrumental music in churches, mentioned in
Chapter II. We had received an invitation to sing
at a Sunday service, and had accepted. One or
two of the deacons had not been consulted; and,
whether from imagined slight of their important
position, or from conscientious scruples, objected to
our entering the house. They were the weakest
party, but a compromise was effected by which we
were not to defame the singers' seats, and the choir
and orchestra were stationed in the broad aisle.
Some of the congregation had not learned of the arrangement, and I noticed looks of holy horror over-
shadowing many countenances turned towards us.
These were mainly directed to the orchestra, and
especially the big fiddle. At the first sound of the
violins and wind instruments, some of these gazers
started as if the last trump had summoned them. It
was absolutely amusing to note the terror depicted
upon the faces of the worthy brethren and sisters,
whose catechism excluded fiddles, trombones, and
organs from the Lord's house. A venerable lady,
in whose very step indignation triumphed, arose,
and moved out of the church. She was followed by
another, and then a whole "pew full" joined in the
retreat. The disaffected deacons caught the fever,
lifted up their hands in holy horror, and, like so
many Aminidab Sleeks, looked from their eyes, as if
they would speak it, "You are all going to the

devil!" and left the desecrated building. When the tune was finished, about a third of the congregation had gone.

I afterwards heard that there had been a row in that church.

The laughable song called "Johnny Schmolker," which has obtained such a wide popularity, was first sung in public by the "Old Folks." It was given to me by a student in Middletown, Connecticut, with the agreement that it should not be published. It was published, however, without my consent, and somebody must have made considerable money out of its sale.

I have, in the preceding chapters, narrated several incidents without regard to date. The remainder of this chapter will be devoted to the last few weeks of the seven months' tour, when I gave a series of "farewell concerts" previous to the departure of the "Old Folks" for Europe. For that tour I had made unusual preparations, having procured new dresses, patterned after the old fashion, for our appearance in Liverpool. These were also worn during the series of "farewells," — a word, by the way, much abused by actors, and other professionals, who do exceedingly well in making a dozen "last appearances." Our farewell in Baltimore occurred during the exciting times of 1860–'61. The programme was interspersed with patriotic airs, and it was thought proper, in view of the exigencies of the times, to give them "The Star Spangled Banner," written by a Baltimorean, as a specimen of good composition. I was a little startled by the storm it raised. People shouted, tossed their hats in the air, ladies waved their handkerchiefs, while others hissed and yelled with pure secession rage. When the first verse was finished, there was a fresh outburst, which, having subsided, was followed by hisses. These were speedily drowned, and thus the uproar continued. The strength of the opposition was great, but the loyal element seemed to predominate. Many left the hall. The whole of this patriotic air was repeated three times,—"Go home, you —— Yankees!" "Stick to your Psalm tunes!" "Nigger-Worshippers!" etc., etc., mingled with applause greeting us from all parts of the house. The Pennsylvania church affair sank into insignificance beside this demonstration.

At one "farewell" in Baltimore, a Christmas-tree, covered with hundreds of cheap but tempting trinkets, was erected in the hall; and it was announced that all the children in the city should have a present by which to remember Father Kemp. Live rabbits, turtle-doves, and "such small deer," were included in the list; but our accomplished agent had the numbers so arranged that these harmless pets should not fall into bad hands. Many

bushels of toys were in the ante-room, in case of
emergency, and the excitement among both old and
young, to obtain a souvenir of Father Kemp, was
intense. As the numbers were called off, much
merriment was occasioned. "No. 290,"— up steps
a small urchin. "Ah, my boy; there's a toy fiddle
for you! To be sure, the neck is snapped off; but
then, you know, it's *something*, just to remember
good old Father Kemp by. No. 166. A doll,
nearly the size of life. I regret to observe, young
lady, that one eye is gone, but it's all the same to
the doll. No. 957; a jumping-jack." A venerable gentleman in the middle of the house comes
forward and receives his reward. Old ladies frequently asked for a token to remember me by. I
freely gave them all I had, in the shape of anything
that cost from one cent to several dollars, though
the former gifts were more profusely distributed than
the latter. In leaving Baltimore I felt assured that
whatever opinion the adults might entertain of me,
the children were all in favor of Father Kemp.

The "farewells" were continued on the route from
Baltimore to Boston, and the company were never
received with greater favor than when they appeared
on these occasions. The last concert took place in
Tremont Temple, and was attended by an audience
which filled every part of the house. I could but
feel gratified that, after so many years of concert-

izing, we should come back to the very place where we were really first brought before the public, and receive such a cordial welcome, and witness so much satisfaction as was expressed by those in attendance. The visit to England was a hazardous experiment, the company being the largest troupe of Americans that ever crossed the Atlantic. I did not expect the same friendly consideration in the land of John Bull that had always been vouchsafed in America, where the public, always quick and appreciative, caught at once the spirit of the enterprise, and patronized it most liberally. The incidents and the tricks (if they may be so called) narrated in the preceding chapters only serve to show what a manager is liable to encounter; and, if the reader considers that I have been addicted to sharp practice, he may be assured that the boot and shoe business does not call for the exercise of any such trifling irregularities. If, therefore, he is in doubt upon the question whether or not I am an honest man, let him call at No. 794 Washington St., and satisfy himself. But I was bidding a series of farewells to America. Let us say good-by for a while, and pass on to the next chapter.

CHAPTER X.

A VOYAGE across the Atlantic in mid-winter is anything but a desirable experience. Many have a quiet way of disposing of their time while crossing the ocean, — by retiring as soon as they get aboard, and arising in about a fortnight, — that is, when they reach the other side. On the morning of the 9th of January, 1861, the "Old Folks," numbering thirty members, were shipped aboard the steamer "Canada," at East Boston, bound for England. It was a cold and clear day, but the wharf was crowded with friends, parting with whom causes the same emotions the world over. Some shed tears; and, I must confess, I felt more like it myself than I did like smiling. Standing on the steamer's deck, I believe the perilous nature of my enterprise presented itself more forcibly than ever before. I assembled the company of "Old Folks," just before the vessel was ready to start, and, inviting those around us to join, we sang together "Auld Lang Syne." The machinery was put in motion, the farewells were hastily taken for the twentieth time, "Blue Peter" came down, and the stars and stripes went up; and we moved out among the shipping, down past the forts; and, at the entrance of the harbor, dropped the pilot. On we went again; the prominent objects in the city faded in the distance, and we were fairly out to sea. The flags were taken in, and the ship was prepared for a rougher ocean life. Part of the first day was passed quite pleasantly, only a few being obliged to remain in their berths. Soon, however, the wind changed, and we enjoyed "chops" (not mutton), which had the effect to satisfy the appetites of a large number, — at least, they did not appear at the table.

On the 12th we neared Cape Race, where we expected to encounter rough weather, and were not disappointed. The storm-king was abroad during the whole night. The ship rolled heavily, and rode on waves mountain high. The wind howled as I never heard it howl before. The captain was on deck all night, but in the morning the danger was considered over. During the height of the storm there occurred one of those scenes whose disagreeable nature cannot be imagined except by those who have witnessed them. Our experience had a ludicrous side. About four o'clock in the morning a heavy sea struck the larboard side of the ship. The concussion seemed like striking against a rock. Some of the passengers were thrown out of their berths; crockery smashed and rattled; women screamed, and men were pale with affright. Some who had never prayed before knelt in supplication. In the midst of this I heard one of our male singers call out to a friend, "Annie, can you swim?" We were in mid ocean, a thousand miles from land.

The effect was so startling that many who were prostrating themselves on their knees crawled into their state-rooms. He followed the question by offering a reward for the man who wrote "A Life on the Ocean Wave," and other like expressions, which turned the whole scene in his neighborhood into one of the most ridiculous nature. An "Old Folks' concert" had been arranged for one evening, but the heavy sea which upset the crockery also upset our calculations in that matter. For once my entertainment was postponed on account of the weather; but, as it was a charity affair, I do not class the circumstance among my regular operations. The incidents of ocean voyages have been often penned, and I cannot add anything interesting to the fund of general information upon the subject. We had our share of their roughness, without much

of their pleasure. At last we came in sight of land,
and on Monday, January 21st, we were steering
along the Irish Channel in a calm sea, and under
bright sunshine. At 6 P. M. we dropped anchor in
the Mersey, opposite Liverpool, the great shipping
emporium of the world.

Getting through the custom-house was attended
with the usual incidents. Our names were taken,
and luggage examined chiefly for spirits and tobacco. I assured the official that the "Old Folks"
were all cold-water men, and none of them used
tobacco; he must recollect that he was dealing
with Americans of a past generation, with whose
habits the British people *ought* to be well acquainted, as they had frequently visited them. "Let
the 'Old Folks' pass," was the only answer to my
remark. Once on shore, we were besieged by newsboys. Mr. Jarrett had been in Liverpool a week,
endeavoring to stir up the town to the fact that
Father Kemp and his company would arrive on the
next steamer. The newsboys were the first to profit
by the intelligence, for they greeted us with, " 'Ere's
yer Liverpool Post and Mercury, — all about the
'Old Folks' !" I purchased several numbers of the
various journals, expecting to find something flatter-
ing to send to my transatlantic friends. Diligent
search revealed nothing about the "Old Folks," the
only place where they were mentioned being in the

advertisements inserted by Mr. Jarrett. "O you little rogue!" said I. The urchin danced away and shouted, "Hi, Jimmy, look at the old buffer's hat! See them wimmin with balloons on!" meaning their hoops. That was a very pleasant greeting from young John Bull to begin with. On our way to the hotel we stopped to witness one of those puppet-shows so common in European cities, — "Punch and Judy." Of course we were much amused, and that formed the first "sight" which we enjoyed in the tour of observation we had now begun. We arrived at the Victoria Hotel at 7 p. m., where dinner in a separate room awaited us. The waiters were neatly dressed, and with white satin ties about their necks, and evidently regarded us with mingled feelings of awe, curiosity, and respect. We were very hungry, but there was nothing on the table, and the body of waiters moved about in slow and measured tread. The edibles at last came gradually along, and we enjoyed an excellent dinner, which was completed at about 10 p. m. This hotel is a very good one, and was at that time very popular with Americans visiting Liverpool. I suggested to the landlord, however, that the Yankees were very impatient, and it was the fashion among the old folks of New England to see their "vittles" on the tables when they sat down. He took the hint, and

three hours were not habitually passed in dining
after that.

The next morning I went to work in good earnest. I was three thousand miles from home, with
one of the largest concert companies in the world.
We were unknown, and had got to meet and conquer that peculiar prejudice which every true Englishman entertains against everything foreign, and
especially American. The mutterings which preceded actual hostilities in 1861 were heard, and
the secessionists had already captured the cotton
merchants of Liverpool, and held them prisoners.
Hatred of the North and everything Northern increased, and the "Old Folks" were identified with
that section. My first business was to get the ear
of the editors; but I found that a much harder task
than I had anticipated. Mr. Jarrett had almost exhausted his ingenuity in that line, and said a new
hand was demanded. The knights of the quill were
very shy, and evidently took great pride in maintaining a calm, mysterious air, while I explained my mis-
sion, and in doing nothing afterwards to assist me in
fulfilling it. While going the rounds to visit the editors, a coal-cart driver, dressed in costume, exactly
like my concert rig, attracted my attention,— the
same three-cape coat, bell-top hat, and knee-breeches
which I was to show the people. Many of the
women also wore bonnets which looked nearly as

large as my "champion." My heart almost sank within me. My intention in matters of dress was to be *behind* the times.

St. George's Hall had been secured for our first appearance. This is the finest building in Liverpool, and one of the finest in the world. The position occupied by it is the most commanding in the city, being on a platform on the brow of a hill. It once formed part of a heath, used as the vantage ground, from which the town was besieged in the civil war between the Cavaliers and Roundheads. The structure, with its seen surrounding dependencies, stands upon upwards of three and a half acres of land, and in its erection more than four hundred thousand cubic feet of stone were used. The building was begun in 1842, and about twelve years were occupied in its completion. It was designed by Harvey Lonsdale Elms, and the style is Grecian Anglicized. The extreme dimensions are : length five hundred feet by one hundred and seventy-five in width; height in centre one hundred and twelve feet, at south front ninety-five feet, and the actual body of the building from north to south is four hundred and seventy feet long by one hundred and sixty wide. The great hall is capable of seating twenty-five hundred persons, and is lighted by means of ten magnificent gasiliers suspended from the room, each weighing about three-quarters of a ton. One of the largest organs

in the world occupies a prominent position, and organ concerts at low prices of admission have been
frequently given there since 1855.   The cost of the
edifice was about £230,000.

The next day after our arrival we had a rehearsal
in the hall, and made every preparation possible to
have the first concert in England a grand affair.

CHAPTER XI.

AFTER we had rehearsed sufficiently long to get the "hang" of the immense hall, I passed the time in attending to the details for the first concert. That evening we visited in a body one of Mr. and Mrs. Howard Paul's entertainments, which are justly popular both in England and America. The preparations for the first appearance were many and trying. One of the duties was to present every American whom I could find with a ticket to the entertainment. I had already disposed of several hundreds on the steamer Canada, and, with those slipped into the hands of the officers who examined our trunks, which, by the way, expedited their performance amazingly, the complimentaries to the press, etc., about three thousand passes were given away. I was determined to have a grand rush on the opening night, and my object was secured. When we appeared before the audience, we opened

our mouths to a crowded audience. I have never,
even in America, witnessed more genuine enthusiasm at an "Old Folks' Concert." I am not vain
enough to attribute this to the English element in
the auditory, but verily believe, if my eye could
have rested upon them individually, it would have
found most of them wondering what it was all about.
The American and other "dead heads," as they are
familiarly called, were evidently determined not to
permit an indifferent feeling in regard to the singing
of the "Old Folks" to obtain, and the way they applauded was most gratifying to me, and correspond-
ingly astonishing to the "Britishers." As we sang
the last tune, I felt that the public were all right, —
but how about the newspapers? I had my eye upon
a burly, red-faced fellow, who represented one of
the papers, and I frequently saw, or imagined I saw,
during the entertainment, looks of disgust overspread
his beer-redolent face, as some commonplace piece
would elicit enthusiastic applause. He evidently
endeavored to ascertain where the "clique" who admired such trash were seated, for he turned his head
nervously, and often furiously about, and his gaze was
both searching and defiant. I told Mr. Jarrett that
the "old fellow" was displeased, and he must be seen
before I slept. I therefore ordered one of the
"flies,"— made something like a chaise, only they use
boards for a boot instead of leather, as we do, and

as near as I could judge, most of the harness was
under the horse's belly. I was driven to the newspaper office, and, I assure the reader, I felt a little
exercised as I mounted the long, dark stairs and
groped my way along to the editorial room. I was
worried about the construction which would be put
upon this new phase of Yankee assurance and
"cheek." I rapped at the door, and a gruff " come
in!" was the result. I entered, and there sat the
editor, of colossal proportions, at his desk, busily engaged in writing. As I noticed the spiteful slashes
and dashes which his pen made upon the sheet, I
felt that every one was a stab at my pocket and reputation. I truly believed he was giving the concert
"fits." I approached the autocrat, hat in hand, and,
with my knees knocking together, and my body
trembling all over like an aspen, told him I was
"Father Kemp," of the "Old Folks." He continued writing, and, without looking up, said, —

"Well?"

"I have come, sir," said I, "to give you some
ideas, and to get some suggestions from you in regard to my concert."

"Horrible! Horrible! Horrible!" roared the
burly Briton.

If a park of artillery had opened upon me, I do
not believe I should have felt and exhibited greater
terror. He kept on with his writing, and did not

7

deign to even look at me. A glance of disgust, indignation, or scorn, would have been soothing.
While I stood there the vision of thirty people, three
thousand miles from home, dependent upon me,
came up before my eyes. I saw the smiles of satisfaction which rested upon their faces at the close
of the concert turned to looks of sorrow and disappointment, at the breakfast-table to-morrow, the
doors of the hall closed against me, and my English
trip turned into a Liverpool fiasco. I began to feel
the injustice of his criticism, and, nerving myself
to the task, took a chair, uninvited, and sat down,
with a coolness which I believe I had never exhibited before. He looked up in amazement, dropped
his pen, and drew back in his chair. We took a
good " square " survey of each other, which occupied
about a half a minute. At last I spoke, not harshly,
but respectfully, —

" Sir, what is the matter with my concert?"

" You can never sing sacred and secular music at
the same entertainment, and prosper in England, —
never, sir, — never ! "

"But were not the sacred and secular selections
both good?"

" That makes no di'erence. There is the established custom ; you cannot come here and overthrow
the usages of the English people."

"Nothing could be farther from my desire, my

dear sir. I have every respect for the customs and usages of the English people. They are a noble race. It is my boast that I sprung from English stock ; but that has nothing to do with the concert. While the Prince of Wales was in America we sang before him, and he applauded — *applauded* us, sir, — and his approbation was equally divided between the sacred and the secular pieces."

I saw I had made a home-thrust, and the old fellow began to scratch his head and look a little uneasy. Without giving him an opportunity to reply, I continued, —

"We have come here on a tour of pleasure, observation, and study. We came as friends, and do not wish to be treated as public enemies. We desire a little attention. The queen's son had that, at least, from us ; it is in your power to reciprocate."

The countenance of the "Island mastiff," which had been gradually softening, now was made radiant with a friendly smile, and his cheeks shone like the sunny half of two Baldwin apples. He blandly asked, —

"Have you any notices?"

"I have, sir ; thousands of them."

"Will you furnish me with one of your best?"

"I will, with pleasure, immediately."

I bowed myself out of his presence, almost too happy to restrain my emotion. Back to the hotel,

and back again to the office, was the work of but a
few minutes.   When I returned I left upon his table
several "first-rate notices" from the American newspapers, and again took my departure.   The next
morning the following appeared in his journal, —

"THE OLD FOLKS' CONCERT TROUPE. —The first
performance of Father Kemp's Old Folks' Concert
Troupe in England took place last evening at St.
George's Hall, which was filled by a highly respectable and delighted audience.   The entertainment is
really of a very novel and at the same time most
pleasing character.   There is an originality about
the whole affair, together with a display of musical
talent, which renders it quite charming.   The Troupe
comprises thirty ladies and gentlemen, — not 'old
folks,' by the way, but youthful instrumentalists and
vocalists of considerable ability.   They are styled 'old
folks,' not from the fact of their being patriarchs of
threescore years and ten, but from the style of dress
in which they appear, — old court suits of the time
of Charles II. and costumes of subsequent dates,
down to the close of the last century.   Some of the
ladies' dresses were made so long as two hundred
years since ; the costumes generally presented a striking contrast to those in fashion at the present day.
The ladies wore towering combs, puffed hair, short-
waisted dresses with very narrow skirts, and bonnets

large enough for two or three heads. One lady looked out from an enormous bonnet, the materials of which would be sufficient for some three or four dozen of the diminutive articles worn as bonnets in these days. The dress of the gentlemen was no less peculiar. They appeared in the extravagant bell-top and three-cornered hats, excessively short unmentionables with corresponding long straps, hats with next to no brim, coats nearly all skirts, powdered hair, ruffles, and the gorgeous full dress of the period of George I. and II. The music generally is of an unpretending, simple character, but it is not the less beautiful. In fact, the purpose with which the entire programme has been framed is to exhibit the style of music in popular favor in the Old American day. The style in which this music was sung is deserving of all the praise that can be bestowed upon it. The instrumentalists played well in tune, kept their place, and most effectively so. *The vocalization was magnificent.* Never have we heard voices more *beautifully or equally blended;* the effect they produced was truly charming. The vocalists are evidently '*picked voices*,' and their rendering of the harmonized pieces was faultless, the attention to 'light and shade,' so frequently neglected, imparting a beauty to their singing which must be heard to be appreciated. During the interval between the first and second parts of the concert the performers prom-

enaded the avenues between the seats in the body of
the hall, in order that the audience might have a
nearer view of their antiquated habiliments. This
afforded considerable satisfaction, — not unmixed
with amusement, as the frequent peals of laughter
testified, — especially to the fair sex, who regarded
with especial interest the gigantic bonnet referred to,
the excessively anti-crinoline skirted dresses, and the
peculiarly quaint head-dresses of the ladies. One of
the latter wore a dress stated to be two hundred and
five years old, and had been a wedding dress for
many parties. A coat worn by one of the gentlemen
was said to be two hundred years old, and his hat
looked as if it had done service at the battle of Bunker's Hill. We should not omit to state that while
these dresses were looked upon with much interest,
the wearers of them were warmly applauded as they
made the circuit of the hall."

I have nothing to add to the above. I feared to
go and thank the old fellow for his kind notice,
which was printed on all the bills afterwards used in
England. I was very handsomely treated in Liverpool, and remained there eight days, sometimes giving three concerts per day. After our concert at St.
George's Hall, one evening we gave an entertainment to the workingmen, which began at 10 P. M.

.

The crowd was very great, the price of tickets ranging from two to twenty-five cents.

I endeavored while in Liverpool to cultivate the acquaintance of my old friends, the school-children. Having hunted one whole day, I at last found a man who kept a beer saloon, who had some authority in the matter, and told him my story; but no explanation could make him understand that we would sing to the juveniles free of expense.

"The children," said he, " know quite enough now; but how long does your *lecture* last? Won't you take some wine?"

This closed the conversation. I thought such a pig-headed fellow could not be a good judge of wine, so I declined. Very few children attended my concerts in Liverpool, as the reader may judge.

As another instance of English stupidity, I will mention an occurrence, — one of many, which indicated the more than Egyptian (Illinois) darkness against which I was obliged to contend in enlightened Albion. A well-dressed man, with whom I was conversing, said he had a cousin living in America, whom he desired very much to hear from. He then astounded me with the question, —

"How large a town is this America?"

I looked at him until assured that he was in earnest, and then replied that it was a very large place. He afterwards informed me that his cousin lived where the steamer went into America, and presumed I might find him when I went back. I took his address. The above is similar to other incidents which, as I have before stated, were every day occurring. There is not so much ignorance concerning this country there now. The great rebellion made the United States known among a class which had before scarcely been aware of their existence. An Englishman, as a general rule, is one of the most self-satisfied of men. If he is learned, he is satisfied with his kind of information; if ignorant, he is content with his ignorance.

I might write another chapter upon my Liverpool experience, but the reader will doubtless think, with me, that I have dwelt upon the subject long enough. I met many friends there, and was more favorably impressed with the city than I had anticipated I should be. A description of the magnificent docks, and some of the buildings might prove interesting, but I leave them to other hands. After " doing" Liverpool, we visited many places around the city, and then took the North-western Railroad train for London, distant more than two hundred miles.

CHAPTER XII.

London — Its immense Area and dense Population — The Houses of Parliament — London Tower.

FOUND London a pretty large place, and when viewing its vast proportions for the first time, and watching the busy throng hurrying and jostling against each other, I wondered if they had any attention to spare for the "Old Folks." I believe I never felt so small and insignificant in my life as when my eyes first rested upon the immense masses of building material which constitute this great city. London is not at a stand-still, either. The city is rapidly growing, new buildings being yearly erected, so that what were pasture lands and wheat fields a few years ago are now handsome streets. Just imagine that you are at the west side of the city, riding on top of an omnibus, going east; you pass dwelling-houses, shops, churches, hotels, factories of various kinds, great buildings for public and private use, banks, offices, railroad stations, — riding ten miles before you get into the open country again. Or, if you were on the north side, going south, you would ride five

miles before coming to the river Thames; crossing
that, over one of the magnificent bridges, you could
ride three miles further with houses all the way, before reaching an open field.

London covers an area ten miles square, and three
and a half millions of people live here, — more in
number than the inhabitants of Maine, New Hamp-
shire, Vermont, Rhode Island, and Connecticut, put
together! More than three hundred thousand cattle, fifty thousand calves, nearly three million sheep
and lambs, fifty thousand pigs, are consumed here
every year, besides all the wheat, corn, potatoes, veg-
etables, fish, chickens, turkeys, butter, cheese, and
milk. There are about forty thousand tailors engaged
in making clothes, and about fifty thousand women
and girls making dresses. There are thirty-five thousand boot and shoe makers. The stores contain goods
from all countries, — from China, India, Japan, Rus-
sia, Egypt, South America, and the United States.
Vessels are coming and going from all parts of the
world. There is no end of railroad trains, — some
railroads running over the tops of the houses on great
bridges, built of bricks and stone, and as you glide
along you can look down into the houses and see
what the people are going to have for dinner. You
look down upon the busy throngs in the streets;
you are up so high that you are on a level with the
belfries of the churches. And there are railroads

also which run under ground for miles, passing under houses where the cooks are getting dinner over your head.

The Houses of Parliament are among the most magnificent buildings in the world, and few have cost more money than they. As you sail down the river Thames, you see rising above the tops of the houses two tall towers, — one three hundred and twenty feet high, and the other three hundred and forty. Besides these there are many spires on the roof, gleaming in the sunshine. The building covers eight acres of ground, or, as that interesting writer, "Carleton," of the "Boston Journal," expresses it, an area larger than a great many corn-fields or potato-fields in New England. It is built of dark gray stone, very nicely hammered, and there are many beautiful figures chiselled in the rock of leaves, vines, lions' heads, and busts of great men famous in history, and many other forms of beauty. If we were to go inside we might travel from noon till sunset through the halls, rooms, and passages. There are eleven large courts, one hundred flights of stairs, eleven hundred rooms, and more than two miles of passage-ways. The front, which we gaze upon from the river, is nine hundred and forty feet long, richly decorated with statues of the kings and queens of England. Between the windows are panels of stone cut in beautiful flowers and scroll work, and coats of arms, and at each end rise the two great towers. At the west end is the Victoria Tower, eighty feet square and three hundred and forty feet high, with four turrets on the corners, tipped with gold, and golden lances between the turrets.

When the queen visits Parliament in the royal coach she enters this tower, passes up the royal court between statues of St. George, the patron saint of England, St. Andrew, the patron saint of Scotland, and St. Patrick, the patron saint of Ireland; and there also is a statue of herself. It would give you much pleasure to walk beneath this grand archway, rising sixty-five feet over your head, blazing with gold. Here noblemen stand in waiting to receive the queen on great occasions, bowing very low as she passes into the rooms prepared for her reception. The tower at the other end of the great pile is called the Clock Tower, which has four great white dials, thirty feet in diameter, where the golden hands, fifteen feet in length, point the passing hours. I know not how many bells there are in the belfry, but you hear them sweetly chiming, filling the air with silvery sounds, and when the hour comes round you hear one, louder-toned, deeper, and heavier than all the others, striking slowly and solemnly. In the night, when the roar of the city is hushed a little, it is heard miles and miles away.

The chamber where the peers of the realm hold their sessions is lighted by six lofty windows, each pane of glass a portrait of one of the sovereigns of England. Here are paintings in fresco on the walls, — one of Edward III. conferring the Order of the Garter on the Black Prince; another represents the Spirit of Chivalry. There are in the niches of the walls statues of men who laid the foundations of constitutional liberty, such as the people of England and of the United States enjoy to-day; statues of the barons, who, in a green meadow on the banks of the Thames, twenty miles up stream, in 1215, compelled King John to sign the Magna Charta.

You look up to the roof fretted with gold and see that it is divided into diamonds and squares, with symbols and devices of curious design, with coats of arms and monograms. At one end of the hall is the queen's throne, a chair of gold, and the State chair, which the Prince of Wales occupies when here, and another seat, with a cushion of rich crimson cloth, which is called the woolsack, — the seat of the lord chancellor. When the lords are in session they sit with their hats on, which people of the United States would not call very good manners; but then, the lords don't put their feet on the desks higher than their heads, nor spit tobacco-juice on the floor, as it is said some American legislators are in the habit of doing, which is as unmannerly as to sit with one's hat on.

At the east end of the building is the chamber in which the commons meet. The hall leading to it has a great many paintings on the walls of scenes in English history.

CHAPTER XIII.

THE Tower of London is one of the most interesting historical piles in the world. As we descend Tower Hill the walls of the ancient palace rise before us amidst the surrounding mass of more modern buildings. The Tower is the castle of the old kings and queens of England, and is closely interwoven with the principal events in the history of the government of that nation. It was built by William the Conqueror, to provide a shelter for himself and awe the rebellious Britons. There are six towers in the outer ward, called the Middle Tower, the Byward Tower, the Traitor's Gate or St. Thomas's Tower, the Cradle Tower, the Well Tower, and the Develin or Iron-gate Tower, and many others within the enclosure, most or all of them associated with some of the prominent scenes in the conflicts which preceded the founding of the form of government which is so acceptable to the Britons at the present time. The smallest division on the first floor is now known as "Queen Elizabeth's Ar-

mory," a cell being connected with it. It is said
that Sir Walter Raleigh, while a prisoner at the
Tower, occupied these apartments. The Devereux
Tower, in the inner ward, is named for the brave
and accomplished Robert Devereux, Earl of Essex,
the favorite of Elizabeth, afterwards beheaded by
her. He was only thirty-four years of age at his
death. He was executed privately, on the green
within the Tower, in front of the chapel.

The other towers have been the prisons of distinguished persons, like Queen Anne Boleyn, Lady
Jane Grey, etc., confined here previous to their
execution. Inscriptions, generally indicating the
greatest sorrow, and the expectation of certain
death, cover the walls of the different apartments.
During the eight centuries which have elapsed
since the erection of the Tower, it never sus-
tained an attack from a foreign foe, but it has
been besieged many times during the civil wars
which have shaken England. It has been used
as a palace and a prison, and now lives in the
past as the guardian of the interesting relics of the
contests and tumults of by-gone days. It would occupy hundreds of pages to describe the suits of
armor, the crown jewels, and hundreds of other
interesting things within its walls. A visit to the
Tower brings to mind the history of England more
forcibly than any other London experience, with

the exception of a stroll through Westminster Abbey, a description of which is reserved for a separate chapter.

The following description, compiled from one of the · guide-books, which those who enter the Tower are expected to purchase, will doubtless be read with interest, as, besides furnishing a condensed history of the edifice, it presents a notable example of "highfalutin" composition, calculated to impress and interest unsophisticated visitors to the British Isles. .

"FIRST PERIOD.

• "During the Norman and early Plantagenet age, history has recorded the names of few captives of note, who were immured within the fortress. One of the most remarkable was the first state prisoner known to have been incarcerated in the Tower of London, — Flambard, Bishop of Durham. His origin was humble, but his talents made him so useful to William Rufus in carrying out his oppressive system of taxation, that he raised him to the highest offices in the State. Henry I. imprisoned him on his accession, 1100, to please the people; but the wily Flambard contrived to escape, and fled to Normandy. Hugh de Burgh was another captive statesman of this period, but of far different order. This great man and faithful minister, was guardian

8

of the king and kingdom during Henry III.'s minority. Those who envied his greatness prejudiced his sovereign against him, and he was cruelly imprisoned within the Tower dungeons for some time, about 1240. He was subsequently released.

"SECOND PERIOD. — THE FOURTEENTH CENTURY.

"At this time the tower appears in the lustre of that martial glory which was shed upon our country by the royal warriors, Edward I., Edward III., and Edward the Black Prince. The national banners which floated over the Tower were 'fann'd by conquest's crimson wing, and the fortress was filled with captive kings and heroes, — trophies of England's valor.' We especially connect the crested pride of the first Edward with the conquest of Wales, that interesting country upon which we look with a feeling akin to reverence, as the retreat of the early possessors of our beautiful England; the country whose mountains were once 'vocal with high-born Hoel's harp, and soft Llewellyn's lay.' A tragical instance of the irksomeness of captivity to Cambria's mountain chiefs was given in the attempt made by Griffin, the son of the Prince of North Wales, to escape from the Tower. The treacherous rope by which he lowered himself from his turret, broke; and the unhappy prince was found next morning a mangled corpse beneath. His son,

undaunted, soon after did escape, and succeeded to
the principality; but only to fall in battle before
the victorious Edward, who sent his ivy-crowned
head to be fixed over the turret which had proved
so fatal to his father. The names of many Welsh
chiefs are chronicled as having been captives in the
Tower during this period. Morgan David, Llewellyn Bren, Madoc Vaghan, and others, some of whom
died in captivity. Owen Glendower proved in the
reign of Henry IV. (1399) how mighty a spirit still
lingered amidst the mountains of Wales. The expiring effort for independence appears to have been
made by Owen's son, and several chiefs, who were
led captive to the Tower by Henry V., then Prince
of Wales, after the battle of Usk, 1410.

Many a mighty spirit from Scotland, too, chafed
within the dismal dungeons of the royal fortress
during the fourteenth century, and just previous to
its commencement. We must only notice the
names of King Baliol, 1297; of the noble Wallace,
who suffered a cruel imprisonment and terrible
death, 1305; of the Earls of Ross, of Athol and
Monteith; of King David Bruce, 1346; the imprisonment of John, King of France, of his son,
and of many French nobles, and the generous
treatment which they received from the noble
Edward, the Black Prince. The treaty of Brètigny
restored John to his throne in 1360.

"Six hundred Jews were incarcerated in these dungeons during Edward III.'s reign for adulterating the coin of the realm. The monarch, whose prejudice against them was strong, finally banished all of that nation from England, compelling them to leave behind them their immense wealth, and their libraries, so rich in the treasures of science, which were taken possession of by the monasteries. Roger Bacon owed much of his extraordinary knowledge to the Jews' libraries, especially to the gigantic volumes of the Babylonish Talmud.

"THIRD PERIOD.

"The splendor of the fourteenth century passed away, and during the fifteenth a gloomy shroud of darkest deeds enveloped the Tower of London. Edward the Black Prince, the pride and the delight of the nation, was arrested by the hand of death in the glory of his manhood. He left his mourning country fatherless, as sheep without a shepherd; it became the prey of the wolf-like passions of rival factions. When the prince's son, the year after his father's death, succeeded to the crown, he was but a child in age; and, as if the moral energy of the stock had been exhausted in his high-souled father and his brave grandfather, Richard II. remained always a child in character. His imbecility allowed lawless ambition to rage unchecked; and the Tower chronicles record how dismally it wrought in the sons, and sons' sons of Edward III. They show us the royal cousins wresting the crown from each other, and dooming one the other to dungeons and to assassination; and, even causing the valleys and plains of England to flow with the blood of her bravest sons, and this, to gratify the terrible lust of power. This dark period was appropriately commenced with the erection on Tower Hill of the fatal scaffold. The first victim whose blood was shed on that spot was Sir Simon Burley. 'A noble knight I found him,' writes Froissart, 'sage and wise.' One of the most accomplished men of his age, he had been selected by the Black Prince as the companion of his son (Richard II.) and his only crime was faithfulness to his young sovereign; an unpardonable one in the judgment of the king's uncles, the Dukes of York and Gloucester, who, having wrested the power from their royal nephew's hands, wreaked vengeance on all who favored him. Richard's good queen, Anne, pleaded for Sir Simon on her knees with tears, but in vain; he was beheaded in 1388.

The king's weak government produced a general discontent; of which, Henry Bolingbroke, son of the famous John of Gaunt, availed himself to win golden opinions, and easily prevailed upon the nation to accept him as their sovereign. The de-

serted Richard soon after, in the presence of the
chief men of the realm, who were assembled in the
great hall of the palace in the Tower, formally
delivered up the crown to Bolingbroke, with these
words : ' Fair Cousin, Henry, Duke of Lancaster, I
give and deliver you this crown, and therewith all
the right thereto depending.' (Froissart.) The
unhappy king was then conducted to the cells of the
Tower, and afterwards to Pomfret Castle in York-
shire.   A mystery hangs over his death.

" The year 1406 brought a most interesting young
captive to the Tower, — James, eldest son of Robert
III. King of Scotland.   On his way to the court of
France to be educated, the royal child was driven
by a sea-storm to take refuge on English shores,
and he was detained by Henry, and doomed to a
captivity which lasted eighteen years.   Henry,
however, gave him a princely education in his prison lodging in the Tower.   His genius was brilliant,
— his thirst for knowledge intense; and when at
length he was restored to his country and his crown,
he was distinguished for consummate wisdom and
virtue.

" The next royal prisoner in the fortress was our
own amiable and saintly, though weak monarch,
Henry VI.

" The House of Lancaster did not wear their
usurped crown in peace.   The House of York as-

serted their more just claims; and the meek monarch would perhaps gladly have yielded to their prior right.

> "'Gives not the hawthorn bush a sweeter shade
> To shepherds, looking on their silly sheep,
> Than doth a rich embroider'd canopy
> To kings, that fear their subjects' treachery?'
> — *III. Part Henry VI. Act II. Sc. V.*

"But not so Henry's warlike queen, Margaret of Anjou. In 1461, Henry was defeated by the Yorkists, and immured in the Tower dungeons. The victory of Margaret at Wakefield, 1470, again seated Henry on the throne and filled the Tower with his enemies. Habited in a robe of purple his nobles led him to the cathedral of St. Paul in triumph; but he only regained his regal splendors to be shorn of them again in the ensuing year. Edward IV. finally defeated the House of Lancaster at Barnet and Tewkesbury, 1471. Henry was sent back to his prison, and was not long after found dead. His queen pined in a miserable captivity for three years afterwards; she was then released from the Tower. Henry VI.'s son was killed at Tewkesbury by the brothers of Edward IV., the Dukes of Clarence and Gloucester. Clarence himself was the next victim. Having aroused his brother, Edward IV.'s jealousy, he was imprisoned in the Bowyer Tower — and murdered — tradition says, drowned in Malmsey

wine. In 1483, the gay Edward sickened and died.
His youthful sons were committed to the care of
their uncle, the Duke of Gloucester, afterwards
Richard III. The royal children were sent to the
Tower, and disappeared. Tradition says that they
were murdered by Richard's order in the bloody
Tower, and buried at the foot of the N. E. staircase
in the White Tower. An impenetrable mystery
veils their fate.

Lord Hastings, who opposed the evil course of
Richard's murderous ambition, was doomed by him
to instant death, on pretence of his approval of
Jane Shore's practice of magical arts to Richard's
injury. The wicked sentence was executed in front
of St. Peter's chapel. The unhappy Jane herself
was immured in the Tower dungeons, and was only
released to die after years of suffering in extreme
poverty. The battle of Bosworth field at length,
in 1485, terminated Richard's dark career, and
placed his rival Henry, Earl of Richmond, on the
throne. Amidst all this darkness we discern glim-
merings of a new dawn : in the previous century,
the pure fountains of life and truth had been un-
sealed through the instrumentality of Wyckliffe.
Truth ever shines as a light, and some were attracted
by its loveliness; but many, alas! found darkness
more congenial, and used their every energy to
preserve it. Thus, in the year 1401, a law was

passed empowering the bishops to imprison any one suspected of *heresy*. From that time, the cells of the Tower were constantly tenanted by those to whom truth was dearer than this world's liberty and life; and often were its dismal recesses the scenes of their terrible tortures. Sir John Oldcastle, Lord Cobham, a man no less renowned for his virtues than for his valor, had the honor of being the first person of rank in this country who suffered in this most noble of causes. Henry V. himself had an interview with him in the hope of prevailing upon him to retract his opinions; but finding even royal rhetoric fail, Henry left him to his clergy, who, after imprisoning him in the Tower, sent him to the stake. He was burnt at St. Giles' in the Fields, 1417.

"FOURTH PERIOD. — THE TUDOR RACE.

"The hero of Agincourt, Henry V., left by his early death a young widow, Katherine, daughter of Charles the Simple, King of France. She afterwards married a Welsh gentleman, Owen Tudor. Henry, Earl of Richmond, was the grandson of this pair; hence his claim to be the representative of the house of Lancaster. A claim which the nation's hatred of Richard III. made them the more ready to own. His marriage to the fair Elizabeth of York, Edward IV.'s daughter, thus uniting the

rival roses, completed the general satisfaction. A
short calm ensued; but it was only a gathering of
stren, th for a mighty conflict of a new order that
was about to commence, — a struggle between light
and darkness, in which the confusion was so chaos-
like, that, for a while, it was often difficult to separate the two — to distinguish error from truth.

"In Henry VII.'s reign the last male of the Plantagenets was a captive in the Tower. The young
Earl of Warwick was the son of that Duke of
Clarence who died in the Bowyer Tower. A victim to Henry's jealousy of the Plantagenets, after
spending his life in prison, he was beheaded on
Tower Hill, charged with attempting to escape from
the fortress with 'Perkin Warbeck,' the name
given to a young man who had presented himself
before the nation a few years after Henry's accession. He bore a striking resemblance to Edward
IV. Highly accomplished and of princely bearing, he announced himself to be Richard Duke of
York, the younger of the royal princes supposed to
have been murdered by Richard III. His claims
were favored by the kings of Scotland and France.
Henry committed him to the Tower, and caused
him to be hung at Tyburn. His whole history is
enveloped in mystery. Henry VIII.'s reign may
be divided into three periods : the first includes the
twenty years of his union with Katherine of Arra-

gon, and the ascendency over him of the Romish
party. Rome was then at the zenith of its perse-
cuting spirit. Cardinal Wolsey and Sir Thomas
More, who both drank into this deeply, influenced Henry; and the cells of the Tower were
filled with those convicted of *heresy*, — the epithet
which it is so easy for error to apply to truth.
Henry's passion for the Lady Anne Boleyn changed
the current of royal opinions; and we see the monarch espousing the cause of the Reformation during
the ten succeeding years of Thomas Cromwell's
power. The Tower dungeons were again filled;
but principally with those who withstood Henry's
claim to be head of the church. The most illustri-
ous of these was the gifted, the excellent, the
beloved, and brilliant Sir Thomas More, Lord
Chancellor; and the venerable Fisher, Bishop of
Rochester, whose imprisonment at the advanced age
of eighty seems to have been very rigorous. He
wrote to the secretary, Lord Cromwell: 'I have
neither shirt nor sute to wear but that bee ragged
and rent so shamefully; my dyett also, God
knoweth, how slender it is at meny tymes.' The
tragical fate of Queen Anne Boleyn is well known.
She died in 1536.

"The Romish party regained an influence over
Henry's mind when the capricious monarch withdrew his favor from Cromwell. The Lady Kathe-

rine Howard, a niece of the powerful Duke of
Norfolk, and had inspired the monarch with an extreme passion. This unfortunate young lady was
brought up by her grandmother, the old Duchess of
Norfolk. A young and lovely creature, left in the
princely old mansion without companions suited to
her exalted rank, Katherine was ruined in early
youth by association with the unworthy dependents
of the family. When afterwards introduced at
court, Henry was fascinated by her maidenly and
winning manners. Her portrait by Holbein, at
Windsor, represents her as a fair girl with ruby lips
and bright-blue eyes. Marillac, the French ambassa-
dor, writing to the King of France, describes her as
'a young lady of moderate beauty, but of most sweet
and sprightly manners.' He mentions Henry's de-
votion to her. She wore round her arms the motto
'No other will but his.'. But no sooner was the
unhappy Katherine exalted to be queen, than
the accomplishers of her former ruin seemed to
hover around her like evil spirits. The opposite
faction caught rumors of the sad truth of the errors
of her childhood (for she was but fourteen when
Derham boasted that she was his wife). Many
terrible accusations were made against Katherine
since she had been queen. She was arraigned for
high treason, and brought to the scaffold in 1542.
She died aged twenty. The only proofs offered of

her guilt seem to be the confessions of those under the influence of torture on the rack.

"Two years before, the gifted Cromwell had perished on Tower Hill. His father was a blacksmith. Spurning this humble employment, he travelled to Rome; became Cardinal Wolsey's steward, then his secretary, and a member of parliament. Introduced to Henry, whose discernment made him appreciate his exalted talents, he was speedily raised to the highest offices in the kingdom. He was a zealous friend of the Reformation; caprice and the rising influence of an opposing party made Cromwell's fall more rapid than his rise. He was seized in the council chamber of Westminster on some frivolous charge of treason, committed to the Tower, and beheaded on Tower Hill in the summer of 1540.

"After his death, no one remained who had power to stem the torrent of persecution of the Reformers as Cromwell ever did. The Tower dungeons were, during the remainder of Henry's reign, filled with learned divines holding reforming views. In 1546, Anne Askew, a lady of cultivated mind and good family, was tortured in the Tower and burnt at Smithfield, for having denied, in conversation, the doctrine of transubstantiation. The last of Henry's victims who can be noticed is Margaret, the Countess of Salisbury, the sister of the Earl of

Warwick, and daughter of Edward IV.'s brother, the murdered Clarence. This now venerable lady was the mother of Cardinal Pole. Her crime seems to have been her royal blood. When brought to the scaffold on the green before the chapel, she refused to lay her head on the block. 'So do traitors use to do, and I am no traitor.' A terrible scene ensued, which ended by the headsman dragging the countess by her gray hair to the block. So perished the last of the Plantagenets of whole blood !

"The reign of Edward VI. witnessed the death on the scaffold of two of the young king's maternal uncles, Lord Thomas and Lord Edward Seymour, through the machinations of Dudley, afterwards Duke of Northumberland. Lord Edward Seymour, the Protector, gained the name of the 'good Duke of Somerset.' Somerset House was erected by him.

"Dudley was the son of Henry VII.'s unpopular minister, the lawyer of that name. His insatiable ambition sought to place the wife of his son, Lord Guildford Dudley on the throne, after the death of Edward VI., 1533. The piety, the excellences, and beauty of Lady Jane Grey had made her the object of the veneration of all parties. She was the great grandmother of Henry VII. through the Suffolk family, and her claim to the throne was founded on a law which Northumberland had induced Edward

VI. to make, which set aside the rights of the
Princesses Mary and Elizabeth. Mary, on her
accession, sentenced the youthful pair to be beheaded; Lady Jane on the Green, Lord Guildford
on Tower Hill. The proposed marriage of Queen
Mary to Philip, King of Spain, gave rise to the rebellion of Sir Thomas Wyatt, which brought many
captives to the Tower (those who have left auto-
graphs in Queen Elizabeth's Armory amongst them).
The Princess Elizabeth herself was suspected by
Mary of being in correspondence with Sir Thomas,
and was committed to the Tower, where she was
treated with considerable rigor. Mary even forbade
the visits of some little children who delighted in
bringing the captive princess flowers. Cranmer,
Ridley, and Latimer were all imprisoned in the
Tower before their martyrdom at Oxford; and the
dungeons were filled with those who suffered for the
faith. The most remarkable prisoners during her
reign are mentioned in the accounts of the Beau-
champ and Devereux Towers.

" THE FIFTH PERIOD. —THE STUARTS.

" The Tudor race becoming extinct at the close of
Elizabeth's brilliant career, the Stuarts succeeded
to the throne; but this line of kings was never in
sympathy with the genius of the nation.

" The convulsions into which society was thrown

by the country's efforts to free itself from a yoke to
which it could not bend, brought many captives to
the Tower; but at length the ungenial rule was
rejected, and James II. left England's throne to the
possession of his gifted son-in-law, William, Prince
of Orange.

"Sir Walter Raleigh claims our first notice in
James I.'s reign. He was committed to the Tower,
on *suspicion* of his being implicated in a plot to
place on the throne of England the Lady Arabella
Stuart, the niece of Mary, Queen of Scots. This
lady was imprisoned for presuming to marry; made
her escape with her husband, was recaptured in
Calais roads, and died in 1616 in the Tower, her
reason having given way under the pressure of trial.
Sir Walter Raleigh was released from a twelve
years' captivity the year of her death; he was sent
to Guiana, in South America, to search for gold
mines; but, failing in this, was on his return re-
manded to the Tower, and beheaded 1618, — it is
said, to please his enemies the Spaniards, whose
favor was sought by James, his son Prince Charles
being about to be united to the Infanta of Spain.
Sir Walter's prowess had too often defeated the
Spaniards for them not to rejoice in his ruin. His
talents as a warrior, a statesman, and an author
were great. Amongst the victims brought to the
Tower by the long struggle between Charles and

his parliament, we can only mention the eminent
statesman Thomas Wentworth, Earl of Strafford,
who was sacrificed in the endeavor to stem the torrent of popular opinion, which was rushing towards
revolution; and who was beheaded, to the intense
grief of his sovereign, 1641; also Archbishop
Laud, who was charged with aiding Charles in his
unconstitutional measures, — with preaching that the
king's prerogative was above all law; and with
seeking to introduce popery again into the established church. The aged prelate died on the
scaffold in 1644. During the protectorate of
Cromwell the Tower was crowded with persons
suspected of favoring the cause of Charles II.;
and, after his restoration, many who had been concerned in the death of Charles I. suffered imprisonment and death. In James II.'s reign the Duke
of Monmonth was induced, by the prevailing
disaffection, to lay a claim to the throne, which he
founded on the plea of the validity of his mother's
marriage to his father, Charles II. After being defeated at the battle of Sedgemoor, 1685, he was
captured and brought to the Tower. One fortnight
after, he was beheaded on Tower Hill. Seven
bishops were imprisoned during this reign in the
Tower, for opposing James II.'s attempt to restore
popery in England. The Judge Jefferies, the noto-
rious abettor of that king's tyranny, on the abdica-

9

tion of his master, was brought to the Tower, and ended his life there in captivity.

"Two more convulsive efforts were made by the rejected race in 1715, and in 1745, when that unhappy family made their expiring effort to recover the forfeited kingdom. This last struggle once more stained Tower Hill with blood. As Sir Simon Burley's was the first, so let us trust that the names of Balmerino, of Kilmarnock, and of Lovat will be the last recorded as having perished on that sad spot. These three Scotch lords were beheaded on Tower Hill, in 1746, for favoring the pretensions of the Prince Charles Edward, grandson of James II."

CHAPTER XIV.

Westminster Abbey — A Description of the Venerable Pile.

VISITORS to Westminster Abbey, as well as to the other noted historical buildings of England, are furnished with a guide, at a small price, which gives a fund of information upon all objects coming under the eye. The entrance to the Abbey is at the "Poets' Corner." The fifth page of the Guide contains the following notice, —

"NOTICE.

"ADMISSION.

"Hours of admission, from 10 A. M. until 4 P. M.; and, in the summer months, until 6 P. M. The Poets' Corner, the Nave, and North Transept, are free at all times. To the Chapels — Admission, Sixpence each person. The Chapels of St. Benedict and St. Erasmus are not shown. The tombs in the Ambulatory, through which the visitor is conducted to the several Chapels, are unnoticed by

the guides. The Chapels are not shown during the
hours of Divine Service, — between 10 and 11 A. M.,
and 3 and 4 P. M. The Cloisters are open, free,
during the hours of Divine Service."

From the Guide before-named the following par-
agraphs descriptive of the Abbey are taken. The
painted lights in the numerous windows, representing various scriptural subjects, royal, armorial
bearings, etc., are marvellously fine specimens of
art. One which particularly impressed me was the
gorgeous South or Marigold Window. In the
centre is the word "JEHOVAH," surrounded by
angels; and in the circle of surrounding lights are
thirty-two subjects illustrative of the principal incidents, miracles, and events in the life and sufferings
of the Redeemer. In the twelve lower lights are
subjects from the Old Testament history.

The writer in the Guide says, —

"Westminster Abbey may, not inaptly, be called
the pantheon of the glory of Britain, for it is its
monuments and remains which render the Abbey so
precious to Englishmen and the whole civilized
world. Here lie nearly all our kings, queens, and
princes, from Edward the Confessor to George II.
At the mention of the very name, what a crowd of
thoughts rush upon the mind! Here kings and
sculptors, princes and poets, philosophers and war-

riors, aged men and budding youth, the vulgar great and the author of imperishable strains, have silently mouldered into dust; and enduring marble embalms their memory. Here the rival statesmen are at peace, and the tongue of the orator is mute; here, side by side, rest the crowned head and the chancellor, the archbishop and the actor, the philanthropist and the naval hero, the divine and the physician, the queen and the actress. Here the Roman Catholic magnate has celebrated mass with more than Eastern splendor; and here the Puritan has poured forth his fervent but lowly exhortation. Here the dread sentence of excommunication has been launched forth in all its terrors; and here the first English Bible issued from the press. Here the magnificence and pomp of the regal coronation have followed the solemn and beautiful burial-service for the dead; and here the pealing organ and the swelling choir, reverberating through the lofty gray-grown aisles, attunes the mind to solemn thoughts and sobriety of demeanor.

"This truly noble specimen of Gothic architecture was originally founded in the seventh century, by Sebert, King of the East Saxons, in the year 610; but, being afterwards destroyed by the Danes, it was rebuilt by King Edgar, in 958. Edward the Confessor again rebuilt and enlarged the Abbey in 1245, and commenced building the present church,

which was continued by Edward I. as far as the
extremity of the choir; the nave and east part were
erected in succeeding reigns, but the most remarkable addition made to it was the Chapel of Henry VII.,
which, though in itself an architectural gem une-
qualled in England, does not harmonize with the
original design.

"In the general plunder of monasteries and
church property, which distinguished the reign of
Henry VIII., Westminster Abbey suffered severely;
but it was treated still worse by the Puritans, in the
great civil war, it being used as barracks for the
soldiers of Parliament, who wantonly destroyed and
mutilated many of the tombs and monuments that
adorned the various chapels; the altars in the
chapels to the saints were thrown down, the images
broken, and the rich stained windows shattered into
fragments.   The restoration of this great national
edifice was intrusted to Sir Christopher Wren, who
performed his task with such ability that the building
was greatly improved, both in solidity of structure
and majesty of effect, he having added the two
towers at the west end.

" 'These towers,' says the poet Gray, 'are after
the designs by Sir Christopher Wren, who also
made drawings of a spire of twelve sides, which is
to be built hereafter.   Neither this master nor the
great Inigo Jones are at all to be admired in their

imitations of the Gothic styles. This front of the Abbey has no detached columns, or other pierced works of carving, to which the true Gothic owes its lightness; and there is, besides, a mixture of modern ornaments entirely inconsistent with this mode of building; such as the broken scroll pediments supported by consoles, with masks and festoons, over the ward apertures, designed for the cornices over the great door, etc. In all the flank views of the edifice the two towers seem to unite, and appear as one square, low, and heavy steeple.'

"During the progress of this re-edification, several curious and ancient monuments were brought to light, which may still be seen; amongst others, the mosaic pavement, executed under the direction of Richard de Ware, Abbot of Westminster, in 1360, now in front of the altar in the choir.

"The best view of the interior is obtained from the great western door. The body of the church presents an impressive appearance, the whole design of the edifice being at once opened to the view of the spectator, with its lofty roof, beautifully disposed lights and long arcade of columns. These pillars terminate towards the east in a sweep, thereby inclosing the Chapel of Edward the Confessor in a kind of semicircle, and excluding all the rest. On the arches of the pillars are galleries of double columns, fifteen feet wide, covering the side aisles,

and lighted by a middle range of windows, over
which there is an upper range of larger windows;
by these, and the under range, with the four capital
windows, the whole fabric is so admirably lighted
that the spectator is never incommoded by darkness,
nor dazzled by glare.

"The coronation of all the kings and queens of
England has taken place in the Abbey; and even
when a monarch had been crowned previously in
another place, as in the case of Henry III., whose
coronation took place at Gloucester, it was thought
proper to have the ceremony again gone through at
Westminster, in the presence of the nobles and the
chief ecclesiastical dignitaries of the land, the archbishop always officiating in the august ceremonial.

"The solemn offices of crowning and enthroning
the sovereigns of England takes place in the centre
of the sacrarium, and beneath the lantern is erected
the throne at which the peers do homage. When
the crowns are put on, the peers and peeresses put
on their coronets, and a signal is given from the top
of the Abbey for the Tower guns to fire at the same
instant.

"Henry VII.'s Chapel, which adjoins the east
end of the Abbey Church, and communicates with
the Ambulatory by a flight of several steps, was
erected by the monarch whose name it bears, as the
place of sepulture for himself and the royal blood

of England; and, till the reign of Charles I., no person but those of royal blood was suffered to be interred there. It was commenced in 1503, the first stone having been laid by John Islip, Abbot of Westminster, in the presence of that monarch, and completed in 1512; and is one of the most exquisite specimens of florid Gothic in the world. The exterior is adorned with fourteen octagonal towers, jutting from the building in different angles, and ornamented with a profusion of sculpture. Its cost is said to have been £14,000, equal to £200,000 of our present money. During a period of eleven years (from 1809 to 1822) the exterior of this superb chapel underwent a complete restoration, under the superintendence of the late James Wyatt, Esq., at a cost of about £40,000, supplied by a parliamentary grant.

"In the nave of the chapel are installed, with great ceremony, the knights of the most honorable Order of the Bath; which order was revived in the reign of George I., in 1725. In their stalls are placed brass plates of their arms; over them hang their banners, swords, and helmets. Under the stalls are seats for the esquires; each knight has three, whose arms are engraved on brass plates. The stalls are of brown wainscot, with Gothic canopies, most beautifully carved, as are the seats, with strange devices. The pavement is of black and

white marble, laid at the expense of Dr. Killigrew,
once the Prebendary of the Abbey.

"The principal object of admiration here, both
for its antiquit♦ and its workmanship, is the magnificent tomb of Henry VII. and Elizabeth his
queen, the last of the house of York who wore the
English crown, executed by the celebrated Pietro
Torrigiano, between the years 1512 and 1518. The
surrounding screen, which is wholly of brass and
copper, is one of the most elaborate specimens of
the art of founding, in open work, that exists. It
is ornamented with many devices alluding to his
family and alliances; such as portcullises denoting
his relation to the Beauforts by his mother's side;
roses, twisted and crowned, in memory of the union
of the two houses of Lancaster and York; and, at
each end, a crown in a bush, referring to the crown
of Richard III., found in a hawthorn, near Bosworth
Field, where that famous battle was fought.

"In a fine vault, under Henry VII.'s Chapel, is
the burying-place of the royal family, erected by
George II., but not now used.

"Besides the church, many of the ancient ap-
pendages of the Abbey still exist. The Cloisters
of the foundation remain nearly entire, and are
filled with monuments, many of which are of great
interest. They are built in a quadrangular form,

with piazzas toward the court, in which several
of the prebendaries have houses.

"The entrance into the Chapter-house (built in
1250) is on one side of the Cloisters, through a
Gothic portal, the mouldings of which are exquisitely
carved. By consent of the abbot, in 1377 the
commons of Great Britain first held their parliaments in this place, the crown undertaking the
repairs. Here they sat till 1547, when Edward VI.
granted them the Chapel of St. Stephen.

"Not far from the Abbey stood the Sanctuary, the
place of refuge granted in former times to criminals
of certain denominations. The church belonging to
it was in the form of a cross. It is supposed to
have been the work of the Confessor. Within its
precincts was born Edward V.; and here his unhappy mother took refuge with her younger son
Richard, to secure him from his cruel uncle, who
had already possession of his elder brother.

"To the west of the Sanctuary stood the Eleemos-
ynary, or Almonry, where the alms of the Abbey
were distributed. But it is still more remarkable
for having been the place where the first printing-
press ever known in England was erected. It was
in 1474, when William Caxton, encouraged by 'the
great' and probably learned Thomas Milling, then
Abbot, produced 'The Game and Play of the
Chesse,' the first book ever printed in England."

CHAPTER XV.

HAVE become so much interested in reviewing the sights in tho Tower and Westminster Abbey, that a return to so modern an affair as the "Old Folks'" concerts seems a decidedly tame occupation. Our arrival in London did not occasion any great excitement. The lords and ladies, with their liveried footmen, drove by us as if we were of tho common herd, and cabmen, and drivers of other vehicles, did not stop to note tho presence of tho venerable troupe from tho New World. We had concluded that our stay in London should bo attended with as little unnecessary expense as possible, and a house stocked with a generous larder and four servants had been secured for our reception. The mansion was on Green Street, near Hyde Park. Tho four servants each had a special duty to perform; but tho experiment was a failure. They could not feed us; and the ladies of

140

the company took the reins, or rather, the pudding-sticks, into their own hands, and we soon enjoyed wholesome New England fare. After a month's experience it was concluded that we could do better by the troupe individually-looking out for themselves; and, during the rest of our stay, we got along quite comfortably, though a frequent comparison of notes and bills of fare revealed the fact that the best food in London is not eaten at the hotels.

Our first concert was given at St. James' Hall. It was full of enthusiastic friends, but the treasury was not overburdened with receipts. The fleas were quite numerous in the hall; but a long intermission was taken, so that we had plenty of time to destroy them, — when they were caught.

One of the first objects to be secured was to appear before the queen. I had seen enough of English disposition to know that should the "Old Folks" do that, and have it announced on their bills, a great point would be gained. With that purpose in view I called on Hon. George M. Dallas, the United States Minister, told him who the "Old Folks" were, and desired his assistance. He assured me that he would aid us all that was in his power. Satin tickets of admission to the concert at St. James' Hall were printed and distributed at one of the queen's levees, and all seemed to be going on swimmingly,

when the death of the Duchess of Kent was announced, and the court went into mourning for six
weeks. This disappointment was somewhat allevi-
ated by an invitation from the President of the Crystal Palace Association, who desired the troupe to
sing in that spacious building, he paying our fares,
and furnishing us with a good English dinner. The
proposition was accepted, and the splendid concert-
room at the side of the palace was crowded long
before the time of beginning. The concert was
given, and we received another invitation to appear;
which I consented to do for the sum of $100 per
hour. We sang there several times afterwards at
those rates, but the manager thought that an hour
at a time was as long as any one ought to listen to
our beautiful music. Our costumes caused much
comment among visitors to the palace, and had I
been of a vain disposition I should have felt very
proud to see myself the recipient of so much attention. By giving afternoon concerts at the palace,
and evening entertainments at St. James' Hall,
though we did not grow rich, we were enabled to
gain sufficient means to "live on the country."

The sale of books, containing all our sacred and
secular songs, also netted quite a handsome sum,
—the receipts at the Crystal Palace for the pamphlet
often being quite as large as the money paid us for
the concert. I adopted a bold method of advertising

in the English capital. Twelve men were employed, who were sandwiched between two boards,—one upon the back and one upon the breast,—and they walked about the streets, one after the other. The "notice" upon the boards was: "Father Kemp's Old Folks sing at St. James' Hall every night." These persons travelled about all day, and were paid twenty-five cents, which they considered good wages.

While in London we saw many sights besides those already mentioned, and which the reader may rightly judge were of a very interesting character. We had frequent opportunities to see the queen, who had not then gone into retirement on account of the death of Prince Albert. She was a fine-looking lady. The turnouts in which she appeared were of course magnificent. In her stable were two hundred horses, besides many ponies for the use of the little princes and princesses. The state carriage is a gorgeous vehicle, which cost £27,000, and is used only on great state occasions, when it is drawn by eight beautiful cream-colored horses.

I called on Mr. George Peabody, the American banker and philanthropist, and transacted my financial business with him. He is a safe man to deal with.

One very interesting exhibition in London was that of Madame Tussaud & Sons, in Portman Square,

of nearly four hundred wax figures, and many interesting relics of historical characters. Madame Tussaud knew how to advertise her "wax-figgers." In
the title-page of the catalogue was the bait at which
every Englishman was expected to bite, and doubtless the flunkeys (all Englishmen, however, are not
flunkeys) considered those names a sufficient guar-
anty of the excellence of the "show." The an-
nouncement read : "Patronized by His Royal Highness, Prince Albert, and the Royal Family; the
Ex-Queen of the French ; Maria Christina, Ex-Queen
of Spain ; Her Royal Highness, the Duchess of Bra-
bant ; His Grace, the late Duke of Wellington, etc. ;
by their late Majesties, Louis XVI., Maria Antoi-
nette, Louis XVIII., Charles X.," etc., etc. The
exhibition was first opened at the Palais Royal,
Paris, in 1772, and appeared in London in 1802. I
tried to get a similar string of titles to affix to my
pamphlet, and at one time seriously thought of
appending to it : Patronized by the Millionnaires of
Reading ; the Dukes of Gloucester and Marblehead ;
the Shoe-makers of Lynn ; the Mayor of Hull ;
Daniel Pratt, the great American Traveller, and
George Washington Mellen, his rival candidate for
the Presidency ; the Sons of the Pilgrims and the
Knickerbockers ; Lo, the poor Indian ; John Smith,
Pocahontas, and other transatlantic notables ; and
perhaps I should, could I have secured permission.

The figures are numbered, and a brief sketch of each personage is given in the book. In that of Prince Frederick William of Prussia, husband of Queen Victoria's daughter, is this statement: "His Royal Highness having been honored with the hand of the Princess Royal of England, received the highest mark of approbation that could be conferred on mortal."

Notwithstanding my inability to make a flourish of trumpets in regard to the distinguished persons who had visited the "Old Folks," I had no fault to find with my patronage in London, as I did not expect to make money there. We sang in various places, and always with good success, so far as applause was concerned. At the Royal Surrey Gardens, we appeared at one end of the hall, while at the other the beer-drinkers and smokers enjoyed their luxuries together with the music. The rest of my London experience can be "better imagined than described." There is one peculiarity about concert-giving in "perfidious Albion," which should be mentioned for the benefit of those who may go there hereafter with the expectation of making money: They are liable to perform before a very large and enthusiastic audience, and get themselves into a fever of excitement with the belief that the treasury is as full, in proportion, as the house. Let them take warning from me, when I tell them that, frequently five hundred people will scarcely yield five hundred pennies to the treasury of the expectant showman. I never saw any one in England who would not take whatever was offered him in the way of a complimentary ticket, or anything else complimentary. There are many people there, I am aware, who are free from this aspersion, but they did not, as a general rule, attend my concerts, — that is, judging by the receipts on many occasions. Aware of the peculiar traits of the inhabitants, I could not do otherwise than gratify their desires, and, consequently, the audiences at my concerts were frequently composed of the jolliest lot of "dead-heads" that ever figured at an entertainment. But I do not begrudge the anxiety I experienced on that account. They at least learned something; and when I have taught an Englishman anything, I feel as if I were entitled to some public praise for having accomplished the feat.

CHAPTER XVI.

ONE of the most interesting places which we visited in England was the city of Chester, a brief mention of whose history will prove far more interesting to the reader than anything I can write concerning the performances of the "Old Folks." I am indebted for most of the facts in relation to this remarkable city to Roberts's Chester Guide, revised by John Hinklin, editor of the "Chester Courant." The city is situated on the river Dee, and should be visited by all Americans who visit England, for pleasure and information.

"There are but few places, if indeed there are any, which can present such varied attractions to the antiquary as this remarkable and ancient city. It is rich in memorable incidents and associations. It has a history chronicled not only in books, but in its walls, towers, rows, and venerable remains.

"'The origin of Chester is of very remote date. No definite conclusion has been reached respecting the exact time of its foundation. Various hypotheses have been started, some of them grotesque and ridiculous enough, but its origin is lost in those mists of antiquity where history fades into fable.

"It is quite clear, as an authenticated matter of fact, that Chester was in very early possession of the Romans. It was the head-quarters of the 20th Legion, which, we find, came into Britain before the year 61; for it had a share in the defeat of Boadicea by Suetonius. After that important victory, this mighty and intrepid people marched onward towards North Wales, and established their authority in Cheshire.

"Scattered through the city have been discovered many vestiges of their power, which enable us to trace their history with considerable distinctness. Wherever they planted their settlements, they left permanent records of their greatness and skill. Many of these memorials have been discovered, in various parts of the old city; and through the intelligent and zealous investigations of the Chester Archæological Society, these antiquities are now made tributary to the instruction of the inhabitants respecting the history of their own locality.

"Not only to the antiquarian, however, is Chester interesting; there is scarcely any order of mind or taste but may here find its gratification. Its noble arched bridge, venerable cathedral and churches,

unique rows, and ancient walls encompassing the
city, with a considerable number and variety of
relics, all combine to make Chester an attractive
place of resort. It is the metropolis of the county
palatine of that name, and is pleasantly situated
above the river Dee, on a rising ground. Its names
have been various. Its Roman name was Deva, undoubtedly, because of its being situated on the river
Dee. Then Cestriæ, from Castrum, 'camp;' and
Castrum Legionis, 'the Camp of the Legion.' Its
British names were Caer Lleon, 'the Camp of the
Legion;' and Caer Lleon Vawr, or Ddyfrdwy,
'the Camp of the Great Legion on the Dee.'

"During the brilliant lieutenancy of Julius Agricola, A.D. 85, it became a Roman colony; and the
place was called from them and from its situation,
Colonia Devana. This is clearly demonstrated by
a coin of Septimus Geta, son of Severus, which had
this inscription : —

'Col. Devana, Leg. xx. Victrix.'

"For two or three centuries after this date, Chester
appears to have continued undisturbed in the power
of the Romans; during which period 'it was a centre of operations while conquest was being produced ;
a centre of civilization and commercial intercourse
when the dominion of the empire was established.
The actual form of the city, its division by streets

into four quarters, exhibits the arrangement which the Romans established in their camp, and which they naturally transferred to the cities which took the place of their military stations. Traces of the work of that wonderful people still remain on our walls, and on the rocky brows which surround them; and excite the attention, and reward the diligence of the antiquarian. Those pigs of lead, the produce of Roman industry, which are first mentioned, in " Camden's Britannia," as being found in the neighborhood of Chester, and two of which have recently been discovered, are memorials of the early period at which the mineral wealth of this district was known, and of the commerce to which it gave rise.' It is a fact, clearly established by history, that to the Romans we are greatly indebted for the introduction of a much higher order of civilization than that which they found existing when they took possession of the country. They were the pioneers of social and religious progress. Previous to the Roman invasion the inhabitants were unacquainted with the laws and arts of civilized life, — painted their bodies, — despised the institution of marriage, — clothed themselves in skins, — knew very little of agriculture, — were furious in disposition, and cruel in their religious superstitions. We find that the practice of human sacrifices was very general amongst them, and in every respect their social and moral condition rude and barbarous in the extreme. So wedded were they to their idolatrous worship and cruel rites, that the Romans, after their conquest, found it necessary to abolish their religion by penal statutes ; an exercise of power which was not usual with these tolerating conquerors. About the year 50, the Emperor Claudius Cæsar subdued the greater part of Britain, and received the submission of several of the British states who inhabited the south-east part of the island. The other Britons, under the command of Caractacus, still maintained an obstinate resistance, and the Romans made little progress against them until Ostorius Scapula was sent over, in the year 50, to command their armies. This renowned general found the country in a state of great excitement and dissatisfaction, but speedily advanced the Roman conquests over the Britons ; defeated Caractacus in a great battle, took him prisoner, and sent him to Rome, where his magnanimous behavior procured him better treatment than those conquerors usually bestowed on native princes. He pardoned Caractacus and his family, and commanded that their chains should immediately be taken off.

"Holinshed is of opinion that Ostorius Scapula was the founder of Chester, and the reasons he adduces are certainly very plausible. He says : 'It is not unlike that it might be first built by P. Ostorius

Scapula, who, as we find, after he had subdued
Caractacus, King of the Ordonices, that inhabited
the countries now called Lancashire, Cheshire, and
Salopshire, built in those parts, and among the
Silures, certeine places of defense, for the better
harbrough of his men of warre, and keeping downe
of such Britaines as were still readie to move rebellion.'

"Passing over the space of a few years, we find
Julius Agricola completing the conquest of this isl-
and.   Such was his formidable power and skilful
policy in governing the people, that we are told they
soon became reconciled to the supremacy of the
Roman arms and language.   He quelled their ani-
mosity to the Roman yoke, and certainly did very
much for the progress of the people in civilization,
knowledge, and the arts of peace.

"There is perhaps no place in the kingdom that can
boast of so many monuments of Roman skill and ingenuity as Chester ; but as these will be described in
detail as we proceed, we need not specify them here.

" About the year 448 the Romans withdrew from
the island, after having been masters of the most
considerable part of its territory for nearly four
centuries, and left the Britons to arm for their own
defence.   No sooner, however, had the Romans
withdrawn their troops, than the Scots and Picts in-
vaded the country with their terrible forces, and

spread devastation and ruin along the line of their march. These vindictive and rapacious barbarians, fired with the lust of conquest, made a pitiless onslaught upon the property and lives of the people. The unhappy Britons petitioned, without effect, for the interposition of Rome, which had declared its resolution forever to abandon them. The British ambassadors were entrusted with a letter to the legate at Rome, pathetically stating their perilous dilemma, and invoking their immediate aid.

"The intestine commotions which were then shaking the Roman empire to its centre prevented the masters of the then world from affording the timely aid sought at their hands.

"Despairing of any reinforcement from Rome, the Britons now invoked the aid of the Saxons, who promptly complied with the invitation, and under Hengist and Horsa, two Saxon chiefs, who were also brothers, wrested Chester from the hands of the invaders. The Saxons, perceiving the weakness of their degenerate allies, soon began to entertain the project of conquering them, and seizing the country as their spoil. During the conflict which ensued between the Britons and the Saxons, who from allies became masters, Chester was frequently taken and retaken, and suffered severely in various sieges. Ultimately, the Aborigines were totally subjugated under the mightier sway of Saxon arms.

"In 607 Ethelfred, King of Northumbria, waged a sanguinary battle with the Britons under the walls of Chester, whom he defeated.

"It is recorded that he came to avenge the quarrel of St. Augustine, whose metropolitan jurisdiction the British monks refused to admit. Augustine is said to have denounced against them the vengeance of Heaven, for this reason, three years previously.

"Sammes, in his Antiquities of Britain, gives an interesting statement of this celebrated battle: 'Edelfrid, the strongest King of the English, having gathered together a great army about the city of Chester, he made a great slaughter of that nation; but when he was going to give the onset, he espied priests and others, who were come thither to entreat God for the success of the army, standing apart in a place of advantage; he asked who they were, and for what purpose they had met there? When Edelfrid had understood the cause of their coming, he said, "If, therefore, they cry unto their God against us, certainly they, although they bear no arms, fight against us, who prosecute us by their prayers."'

"The victory was not destined, however, to be an abiding one. The supremacy of Ethelfrid over the Britons was not long in duration. History tells us that a few years after he had achieved his conquest, the united forces of Brocmail and three other British princes rescued from his hands the possession of Chester, and put his armies to flight. In 613 the Britons assembled in Chester and elected Cadwon their king, who reigned with great honor for twenty-two years.

"From this period to the close of the Heptarchy, we have but very scanty materials respecting the history of Chester. The Britons appear to have retained possession of it until about the year 828, when it was finally taken by Egbert, during the reign of the British prince Mervyn and his wife Esylht.

"In a few years afterwards (894 or 895) the city underwent a heavy calamity, from its invasion by Harold, King of the Danes, Mancolin, King of the Scots, and another confederate prince, who are said to have encamped on Hoole Heath, near Chester, and, after a long siege, reduced the city. These predatory pirates were soon after attacked and conquered by Alfred, who utterly routed them from the military defences in which they had embosomed themselves, and destroyed all the cattle and corn of the district.

"After the evacuation of the city by the Danes, it remained in ruins until about the year 908, when it was restored by Ethelred, the first Earl of Mercia, and Ethelfleda, his wife, who, it is said, enlarged it

to double the extent of the Roman town. Sir Peter
Leycestor says that 'Ethelred and his countess restored Caerleon, that is Legecestria, now called
Chester, after it was destroyed by the Danes, and
enclosed it with new walls, and made it nigh such
two as it was before; so that the castle that was
sometime by the water without the walls, is now in
the town within the walls.' All the narratives
which have been handed down to us of this celebrated
woman represent her as possessed of incomparable
talent, great enterprise, and pure mind. She employed the great power and opportunity she possessed
with admirable wisdom, and made them subservient
to acts of munificence and piety. She died at Tam-
worth in 922, whence her body was translated to
Gloucester. Leycestor gives a lengthy record of her
good deeds, which prepares us for the fact that her
loss was deeply and universally regretted throughout
the whole kingdom.

"The security of Chester against the Danish invaders was ultimately effected by the victories of
Edmund, in and about 942, after which it was occasionally honored by the residence of the Saxon
sovereigns. Pennant says, King Edgar made this
one of the stations in his annual circumnavigation
of his dominions. About the year 973 he visited
Chester, attended by his court, and received the
homage of his vassal kings. It is said that one day,

entering his barge, he assumed the helm, and made his eight tributary princes row him from the palace, which stood in the field at Handbridge, opposite the castle (and which still bears his name), up the river Dee, as far as the monastery of St. John's. In the following century Chester was possessed by the Earls of Mercia, until the Norman Conquest in 1066. The tyranny, violence, and bloodshed which marked the course of William the Conqueror met with determined resistance in various parts of the country; but in the course of six or seven years he utterly crushed all opposition, and became absolute master of the island. He introduced into England the feudal system, 'with its military aristocracy, its pride, its splendor, and its iron dominion. The importance of Chester as a military station was shown by its being assigned as a fief to one of the chief leaders in the Norman army, and on his death by its being given to the nephew of the duke himself, under whom it was invested with privileges which raised it almost to the rank of a separate principality. Under Hugh, the first Earl of Chester, and his immediate successors, we may suppose that most of those castles were built, which form objects of antiquarian research in the neighborhood, but which are melancholy records of the state of society at the time, since they were evidently built to protect the frontiers from the continued invasions of the Welsh.

Some of them still remain, and, from their extent and magnificence, appear to have been the residences of the earls themselves. Many more have perished, and can only be traced by the banks which mark the outline of their plan. These were probably of an inferior description, and are rather to be considered as guard-houses for the protection of some particular pass, than as regular fortresses. There are traces of this kind at Doddleston, at Pulford, at Aldford, at Holt, at Shotwick, besides the larger and more distinguished holds at Beeston, Halton, Chester, and Hawarden; and probably few years passed but that some inroad of the Welsh carried fire and slaughter to the very gates of Chester, and swept the cattle and produce from the fields.' *

"For many years previous to the Norman Conquest Chester was governed by dukes or earls; but William, perceiving the danger of entrusting so large a territory in the hands of any one of his barons, curtailed the provinces within narrower limits, and thereby crippled the power which had often proved dangerous to the throne, and at the same time augmented his own, by having a larger number of gifts and emoluments to bestow on his followers. In the first instance William gave Chester to Gherbodus,

* Rev. Chancellor Raikes' Introductory Lecture before the Chester Archæological Society.

a noble Fleming, who, having obtained permission of the king to visit Flanders for the transaction of some private business, there fell into the hands of his enemies, and was obliged to resign the earldom to Hugh Lupus, the nephew of the Conqueror, who was appointed in his stead. The earldom was now erected into a palatinate. Camden says, 'William the 1st created Hugh, surnamed Lupus, the first Earl of Chester and Count Palatine, and gave unto him and his heirs all the county, to be holden as freely by the sword as the king himself held England by his crown.'

"By reason of this grant the Earls of Chester were invested with sovereign jurisdiction, and held their own parliaments. It is supposed that Lupus was invested with his new dignity at Chester by William himself, when he was present there in person in 1069.

"The Earls of Chester continued to exercise their local sovereignty for about one hundred and sixty years. They held that sovereignty, it is true, as the representatives of the paramount sovereignty of the King of England, and as owing allegiance to him in all things; but so far as the government of the Palatinate was concerned, their rule, though nominally mediate, was actually absolute, for the king does not appear to have thwarted their jurisdiction, or in any way to have exerted his supreme authority, beyond retaining a mint at Chester.

"After the death of the seventh Earl, in 1237,
Henry the Third united the earldom to the crown;
he afterwards conferred it upon his eldest son,
Prince Edward, about A.D. 1245, who, two years
after this, received the homage of his military tenants at Chester. From that period to the present
the title of Earl of Chester has been vested in the
eldest son of the reigning sovereign, and is now
held by His Royal Highness, Albert, Prince of
Wales.

"In 1255 Llewellyn ap Gryffid, Prince of Wales,
provoked by the cruel injuries his subjects had received from Geffrey Langley, Lieutenant of the
County under Prince Edward, carried fire and sword
to the gates of Chester. In 1257 Henry the Third
summoned his nobility and bishops to attend, with
their vassals, at Chester, in order to invade Wales;
and in 1275 Edward the First appointed the city as
the place for Llewellyn to do him homage, whose
refusal ended with the ruin of himself and his principality; for in 1300 Edward of Carnarvon here received the final acknowledgment of the Welsh to
the sovereignty of England; and in a few years
afterwards, Llewellyn was brought hither a prisoner
from Flint Castle. Richard the Second visited this
his favorite city in 1397, and in 1399 he was brought
a prisoner from Flint Castle to the castle of Chester,

which Bolingbroke, afterwards Henry the Fourth, had seized.

" In Owen Glendower's wars this city was a *place d'armes* for the English troops in the expeditions against the Welsh, who, ever tenacious of their independence, were as unwilling to submit to the Norman as the Saxon yoke.

" In 1459 Henry the Sixth, with Queen Margaret and her son Edward, visited Chester, and bestowed little silver swans on the Cheshire gentlemen who espoused her cause.

" It appears that Henry the Seventh and his queen also visited Chester in 1493. In 1554 George Marsh, the pious martyr, was publicly burnt at Boughton, for his steadfast adherence to the Protestant faith. In the year 1617 the city was honored with the presence of James the First, when Edward Button, the then mayor, presented the king with a gilt cup containing one hundred jacobuses of gold.

"From this time no event of any great importance appears to have transpired, until the city was involved in the calamities of a siege, in consequence of its loyalty to Charles the First. The city stood the siege for some months; but the inhabitants at last, reduced to the extremity of famine, so that they were compelled to eat horses, dogs, cats, and other animals, abandoned their resistance, made

11

honorable terms of capitulation, and yielded the city on February the 3d, 1645-6.

"Chester was, probably, in the time of the Romans, or earlier, a thriving port. The Saxon navy was stationed here, and it was also the seat of the Mercian kings. About the time of the conquest the imports and exports appear to have been considerable. But as an illustration of the times we may mention, that one article of the latter was slaves, obtained, it is conjectured, from the captives which were made in the frequent wars with the Welsh. It is quite clear that Chester was, in ancient days, a busy and flourishing port, because of the perfectly navigable condition of the Dee. All the early writers of its history unite in bearing testimony to this point. It may here be mentioned, as a curious and interesting fact, that some centuries ago, Flookersbrook was covered with water, and that a deep and broad channel flowed through Mollington, Stanney, and that direction, which emptied itself into the estuary now called the Mersey. Holinshed, after tracing minutely the course of the Dee through Flookersbrook up to Stanney, distinctly states that it 'sendeth foorth one arme by Stannie Poole, and the Parke side into Merseie arme,' etc. Speed distinctly marks out this course in his map; and it is still more broadly defined in an old Dutch map, of a much earlier date, printed at Rotterdam.

"In consequence of the uncertain and imperfect state of the river, the once thriving commerce of this ancient port has dwindled into comparative insignificance, and Liverpool has reaped the advantage. Spirited efforts have latterly been made to improve the navigation and port of Chester.

" The first charter granted to the city was by the first Ranulph, also styled Ranulph le Meschin, third Earl of Chester, who died in 1128. It grants to his tenants demesne of Chester, that none but they or their heirs shall buy or sell merchandise, brought to the city by sea or land, except at the fairs holden at the nativity of St. John the Baptist, and on the feast of St. Michael; and is directed thus — Ranul. com. Cestræ. constabulario. dupifero justiciar. vicecom. baron. militibus bullivis et omnibus servientibus suis præsentibus et futuris, salutem; Sciatis, etc. ; and so makes a large grant to the city, and warrants the same strongly against his heirs, and appoints forfeitures upon all that shall withstand. The charter, which is without date, is witnessed by Domino Hugone, Abbate Cestriæ; Domino Hugone le Orebi, tunc. justiciar; Warren de Vernon, etc., etc. It was confirmed by the other two Earls Ranulphs, and also by Earl John, who strictly prohibited all buying and selling except as aforesaid, with other additions. King John and Henry the Second also established it, with the addition of some further privileges. Henry the Third granted three charters, in the first of which he recites, that he hath seen the former charters of the earls, and doth grant and confirm domesticis hominibus Cestr. etc., that none shall buy or sell merchandise in the city, but citizens, except in the fairs, etc., sub pœna £10.

"It was at this time that, so far as we can ascertain, the first mayor was created.* In the 26th year of Henry's reign, Sir Walter Lynnet was the first who was invested with civic honors and authority. The mayoralty of Chester is, therefore, a very ancient one, — only fifty-eight years younger, we believe, than that of London.

" In 1300 Edward the First confirmed the former charter of his father, Henry the Third; and by the same charter gave the city of Chester, with the appurtenances, liberties, and freedoms, to the citizens of Chester and their heirs, to be holden of him and his heirs forever, paying yearly £100. He granted them also the election of coroners and pleas of the crown, and that the citizens shall have sock, sack, toll, theme, infangtheof, outfangtheof, and to be free throughout all the land and dominion of toll, passage, etc.

" Many other charters follow, and other matters connected with the government of the city.

"Richard the Second, in 1347, 'for the further-

* Ormerod's Cheshire, page 173.

ance of justice and better execution thereof, grants unto his subjects, maiors, sheriffs, and commonality of the said city, to hold their courts; and limited what processes they may award in actions, personal felonies, appeals, process of uttagary, as at the common law;' and since then the sessions of the peace have continued to be held down to the present time.

"Henry Seventh, 'in consideration that through the decay of the haven and river, by many burstings forth, was become sandy and impassable, as before, for merchandise,' remitteth £80 annually of the fee farm rent. And the said King Henry Seventh granteth that the city of Chester and the suburbs, towns, and hamlets thereof, the castle excepted, should be a county of itself, by the name of the county of Chester.

"Henry the Eighth sent letters in parchment under his privy seal to the Mayor of Chester, charging that the citizens should not be pressed unto the war, but remain within the city for the defence thereof. He also, by letters patent, discharged the city from being a sanctuary for malefactors, which was by proclamation removed to Stafford. In the thirty-second year of the same reign the city obtained the privilege of returning two burgesses as its representatives in the English Parliament.

"Altars, Roman pavements, pigs of lead, coins, and other precious relics of former times, have been discovered in various places in the city and neighborhood, some of them within a very recent period.

"On a projecting rock in Handbridge, situated at the south end of the bridge, is a sculptured figure of Minerva, with her symbol, the owl. Time has very much obliterated and defaced this ancient sculpture, called Edgar's Cave, which is doubtless of Roman date. Close to the figure is a great hole in the rock; and the field in which it is situated is known by the name of Edgar's field to the present day.

"In the year 1653 an altar, supposed to have been dedicated to Jupiter, was dug up in Foregate Street, and which is preserved among the Arundelian marbles at Oxford.

"In April, 1850, whilst excavating for a drain on the premises belonging to Mr. Wynne, carpenter, on the east side of Bridge Street, adjoining the Feathers Lane, a portion of a tile flooring, of mediæval construction, was discovered, in a remarkably good state of preservation. This floor was made the subject of a lecture by Mr. Harrison, architect, which is embodied in the reports published by the Chester Archæological Society. Large square Roman tiles of red clay are frequently found in removing old buildings, and breaking up the pavements, in Chester. Many of these are stamped with the inscription of the 20th Legion, LEG. XX. VV., and others are marked, LEG. VV. Œ.

"These tiles were manufactured by the soldiers of the legion, who were accomplished masons, being trained to use the pickaxe, spade, and trowel, as well as military arms. In times of peace they were employed in building houses and public edifices, constructing roads, and tilling the fields. To them 'we are indebted for nearly all the inscriptions discovered in this country, which abound in the districts where they were regularly quartered or employed on public works, and are comparatively scarce in other localities.'

"A great number of coins have been found at various times within the walls of Chester, of Vespasian, Trajan, Hadrian, Fl. Val. Constantius, and other Roman emperors, some in brass, and others in silver. A very fine gold coin of Faustina the elder, wife of Antonius Pius, was found a few years ago near the castle; and in 1826 a very beautiful gold coin was dug up in a field at the east end of Captain Wrench's house, which is in the possession of Captain Wrench. On the obverse is the head of Nero, with his title, NERO CÆSAR AVGVSTVS, and on the reverse is a figure in a sitting posture, and the legend SALVS.

"Whilst excavating a drain in Grosvenor Street, in 1828, several coins were found, some of which

were in very good preservation, especially one of
Trajan and another of Geta. A lamp made of lead,
and an ivory stylus were also dug up at the same
time. In the same year was found, near the new
church of St. Bridget, a small altar, without any
inscription to assist the antiquarian in ascertaining
anything respecting its dedication. Within the space
of a few inches from the altar was found a brass
medal, on which the figure of the god Neptune is
clearly delineated, with his trident, and a ship with
her sails. The legend on it is NEPTVNVS; on the
reverse is Hercules with his club, and a female
figure by his side, and around is the inscription
HERCVLES ET PALLAS.

"A short time ago a small votive altar was found
by W. Ayrton, Esq., at Boughton, near the spot
where an altar dedicated to the Nymphs was discovered.

"The inscription has been interpreted thus, —

"'GENO. AVERNI. IVL. QVINTILIANVS.'
''Julius Quintilianus to the Genius of Avernus.'

"Examples of dedication to genii are very numerous; the belief that they presided over the welfare
of cities, families, and individuals was part of the
religious system of the Romans. It was generally
believed that every individual had two genii, the
one good, the other bad. With reference to the

particular inscription to the genius Avernus, Mr.
Roach Smith says, 'that he finds no other mention;
but the locality in which the altar was found con-
firms the literal interpretation that the genius of the
well-known lake in Carpania is here to be understood as addressed by Julius Quintilianus.   The
waters of the lake were much used by the Romans
in magical rites, as the classical reader will be reminded by the line in Virgil's description of the
incantation scene, preparatory to Dido's death,—

"'Sparserat et latices simulatos fontis Averni.'

"A short time ago there was found in Common
Hall Street, embedded in a thick wall several feet
under ground, a singular block or pig of lead.

"Unfortunately the inscription has only been par-
tially preserved, inasmuch as it presents a different
reading from others which have been discovered,
and which Camden mentions as being very general
in Cheshire; but those which he records as having
come under his notice had inscribed on them, —

"'IMP . DOMIT . AVG . GER . DE . CEANG.'

"These pigs of lead appear to have been paid as
tribute by the Britons to their Roman masters, 'the
harsh exaction of which was one of the causes of
the insurrection.'

"A great quantity of the red Samian, and other

kinds of pottery, have been discovered within the
walls of Chester, which are supposed to have been
of foreign origin.

" But small portions of the original Roman wall
of Chester now exist, although undoubted vestiges
of that ancient work are easily discernible. The
present wall, no doubt, stands on the original foundation. The Roman pavement has been often discovered at the depth of a few feet below the modern
road, in the principal streets, which, in all proba-
bility, run in the same direction as those of the
Roman city. During the last few years, many remarkable antiquities have been discovered in making
excavations for new buildings; and, among such
remains, a fine Roman altar, bearing a Greek inscription, has excited great interest and speculation.

" The Chester walls are the only perfect specimen
of this order of ancient fortification now to be met
with in England. There is nothing, perhaps, which
impresses a stranger more forcibly, or sooner at-
tracts his interest and curiosity, than these em-
battled memorials of the olden time."

The following is their condensed history, —

" Ancient Roman Walls, city of Chester, varying
from twelve to forty feet in height; built A. D. 61.
A public promenade of nearly two miles around the
city. A. D. 73, Marius, King of the Britons,
extended the walls. A. D. 607, the Britons de-

feated under the walls. A. D. 907, the walls rebuilt by the daughter of Alfred the Great. A. D. 1224, an assessment for repairing the walls. A. D. 1399, Henry of Lancaster mustered his troops under these walls. A. D. 1645, the parliamentary forces made a breach in the walls. These walls have two towers and four gates; viz.: Water Tower, — an addition was built to it in 1322; Phœnix Tower, — Charles the First stood on it and saw his army defeated in 1645; Eastgate, rebuilt 1769; Northgate, rebuilt 1808; Watergate, rebuilt 1778; Bridegate, rebuilt 1782.

"In King's 'Vale Royal' it is stated that they were first built by Marius, King of the Britons, A. D. 73. Leland and Selden, both authors of credit, attribute to the Romans the foundation of Chester. According to Geoffry of Monmouth, Higden, Bradshaw the monk, and Stowe, it is of an origin more ancient than Rome itself, and was only re-edified by the legionaries; but, in support of their assertions, the aforesaid writers, all of whom delight in the marvellous, give no other authority save vague tradition. On the other hand, the walls of Chester, at this hour, bear witness to the truth of Leland and Selden's account of their origin.

"They are built of soft freestone, and command extensive and beautiful prospects. The view from the Northgate, with the Welsh Hills in the distance,

is universally admired. The walls are a mile ar
three-quarters and one hundred and twenty-ol
yards in circumference, and are kept in repair b
the corporation.

"Very curious are the old arcades, which are :
interesting to the antiquarian as they are convenie
for a quiet lounge to ladies and others engaged i
shopping. They occupy the greatest part of bol
sides of Eastgate Street, and the upper parts c
both sides of Watergate Street and Bridge Stree
Those in Northgate Street are more irregular; onl
one side, commonly called Shoemakers' Row, bein
used as a regular thoroughfare. Their appearanc
both interior and exterior, is extremely singula
They form a gallery, occupying the front floor c
each house, parallel with the streets below, and ai
approached by flights of steps, placed at convenier
distances, in addition to those by which they ai
entered and quitted at each end. The passeng
walks over the shops on a level with the street, ar
under the first floor of the dwelling-houses; ar
thus two lines of shops are erected in one fron
The rows are kept in excellent repair, and form tl
chief promenade of the citizens. To strangers the
cannot fail to prove an object of curiosity. Tl
shops in the rows are generally considered the be:
situations for retail traders; but those on the soutl
ern side of Eastgate Street and the eastern side c

Bridge Street, have a decided preference. Shops let here at high rents, and are in never failing request; and there are no parts of the city which have undergone such rapid or extensive improvements.

" In the sixteenth century the rows appear not to have exceeded six feet in height and ten in width, with clumsy wooden rails towards the street; and large oaken pillars, supporting transverse beams and brackets, on which rested the houses overhead, formed of wood and plaster, so far overhanging the street that in some places the upper floors of opposite houses nearly met. Nearly the whole of the buildings of this description are now taken down; and, in rebuilding, care has been taken to raise and widen the rows, and to place iron railings towards the street in place of the wooden posts formerly used. The shops in the rows present a very different appearance to that of about sixty years ago; then, as Hemingway says, 'the fronts were all *open* to the row in two or three compartments, according to their size; and at night were closed by large hanging shutters, fixed on hinges, and fastened in the daytime by hooks to the ceiling of the row.' At present these rows are 'capable of supplying all the real demands of convenience and the artificial calls of luxury, mental and corporeal, presenting a

cluster of drapers, clothiers, jewellers, booksellers,
etc., as respectable as the kingdom can produce.'*
The origin and cause of the rows has furnished
matter for much curious investigation; and many
conflicting conjectures have been propounded respecting them. The subject is involved in much
obscurity; and, in the absence of any positive data,
we are not able to take higher ground than the
probabilities of the case. It has been alleged that
they were originally used as places of defence, from
whence to annoy and repulse the assaults of the
enemy, who might gain entrance into the streets
beneath by surprising the gates, during those remote
ages when Chester was subject to the sudden incur-
sions of the Welsh. But against this opinion it
may be urged, that in no one of their attacks upon
this city did the Welsh ever force their way within
the gates or walls; so that these latter, being proved
by experience to be a sufficient bulwark against our
foes, there existed no necessity for the erection of
any further defences.   There is irrefragable evi-
dence that the *form* of the city is Roman, and that
the *walls* were the work of that people; and the
same reasons which justify these conclusions are not
less cogent for presuming that the construction of
the streets is Roman also. Pennant appears to
have arrived at this conclusion. He says: 'These

* Hemingway's "History of Chester."

rows appear to me to have been the same with the ancient *vestibules*, and to have been a form of building preserved from the time that the city was possessed by the Romans. They were built before the doors, midway between the streets and the houses, and were the places where dependents waited for the coming out of their patrons, and under which they might walk away the tedious minutes of expectation. Plautus, in the 3d Act of his *Mostella*, describes both their station and use. The shops beneath the rows were the Cryptæ and Apothecæ, magazines for the various necessaries of the owners of the houses.'

" Ormerod says that some of these crypts exhibit specimens of vaulting equal to the cloisters of our Cathedral.

" Camden, in describing Chester, says, 'The houses are very fair built, and along the chief streets are galleries or walking-places they call rows, having shops on both sides, through which a man may walk dry from one end to the other.' And Shukeley, in his 'Itinerary,' in 1724, says, 'The rows or piazzas are singular through the whole town, giving shelter to foot people. I fancied it a remain of the *Roman porticos.*'

" In the oldest histories, descriptive of the city in some form or other, the elevated rows and the shops beneath are recognized.

"Tacitus, 'in describing the process by which Roman manners diffused themselves throughout Britain, and gradually completed the subjugation of the country, speaks of the natives of Britain as acquiring a taste for the two leading features in Roman civilization, — "Porticus and Balnea," — the portico, in which they were delighted to stroll and sun themselves; and the baths, which were their national luxury. He mentions these, and we cannot but be struck by the coincidence with things with which we are all familiar, — the *rows* of our ancient city, and the Hypocaust, which is still shown as the Roman bath. We are hereby led to infer that the mode of construction which gives the character to our city originated in Roman habits.' *

"At the corner of the east of Bridge Street and the west of Eastgate Street, and near to the Cross, there was formerly a small stone building, forming a basin at the top, called the *Conduit*, to which water was formerly brought into the city from St. Giles's well at Boughton, and thence conveyed to different parts of the city.

"The Cross used formerly to be the scene of the barbarous sport of bull-baiting, of which the following satirical sketch is given in an old History of Chester, —

" 'The Cross is famous for being the annual scene

* Rev. Chancellor Raikes.

of exhibition of that *polite play* called a bull-bait, where four or five of these *horned heroes* are attended by several hundred lovers of that *rational amusement.* Till within a few years, the *dramatis personæ* of this *elegant scene* included even magistracy itself, the mayor and corporation attending in their official habiliments at the Pentice windows, not only to countenance the *diversions* of the *ring,* but to participate in a sight of its *enjoyments.* A proclamation was also made by the crier of the court, with all the gravity and solemnity of an oration before a *Romish sacrifice,* the elegant composition of which ran thus : " *Oyez! Oyez! Oyez! If any man stands within twenty yards of the bull-ring, let him take — what comes.*" After which followed the usual public ejaculations for "the safety of the king and the mayor of the city ; " when the *beauties* of the scene commenced, and the dogs immediately *fell to.* Here a prayer for his worship was not unseasonable, as even the ermined cloak was no security against the carcasses of dead animals, with which spectators, without distinction, were occasionally saluted.

" 'We shall not attempt a description of the *tender* offices practised, at such times, on so noble a creature. One, however, we cannot omit mentioning. In 1787, an unfortunate animal, smarting under his wounds and fatigue, was very *naturally*

induced to *lie down;* the *argument* made use of, in
this situation, however, *as naturally* induced him to
get up; his *humane* followers hitting upon the
ingenious expedient of setting fire to some straw
under his body, when, it is hardly necessary to add,
" the wretched animal heaved forth such groans as
stretched his leathern coat almost to bursting.'
This circumstance of the *fire* was, however, no bad
satire (emblematically considered) on the transac-
tions of the day ; the whole being little better than
a — " burning shame."

" ' The late Dr. Cowper is said to have had the
merit, when mayor, of putting a stop to the attendance of the corporate body on these days ; and
Mr. Alderman Brodhurst, in his mayoralty, made a
laudable but ineffectual effort to suppress a relic of
barbarism " more honored in the *breach* than in the
observance." '

" The citizens of Chester appear to have been
early distinguished for a love of theatricals.   From
a MS. entitled ' Certayne collections of aunchiante
times concerninge the aunchiante and famous Citty
of Chester,' by Archdeacon Rogers, we learn that
in the beginning of the fourteenth century, Randa
Higden, a monk of Chester, ' translated the Bible
into several partes and plays, so as the common
people might lerne the same by theyre playinge.
These *spectacles,* then called the *Whitsun Plays*

were first performed in 1328, during the mayoralty of Sir John Arneway, at the expense of the city companies; and, being 'profitable for them, for all both far and near came to see them,' they were repeated annually on Monday, Tuesday, and Wednesday, in Whitsun week, for nearly two hundred and fifty years, until 1574, when they were suppressed by authority. The theatre for these performances was of the original Thespian cast, a four-wheeled scaffold or wagon, whereof the body did serve for the tyring room, and the roof for the stage, whereon the members of the different city companies did 'each man play his part.' The first place of performance was at the Abbey Gate, that 'the monks and churche might have the first sighte, and then the stage was drawne to the High Crosse before the Mayor and Aldermen, and soe from streete to streete; and, when one pageant was ended, another came in the place thereof, till all that were appoynted for the daye were ended.' Each company had its own peculiar parts allotted to its members to perform in the Whitsun Plays, of which a list is given in the above quoted MS.

"In addition to the Whitsun Plays, the citizens were anciently entertained with processional pageants by the different companies, which latter appear to have survived the suppression of the former for many years. They were suppressed for some time by the party in power during the Commonwealth, but revived with great splendor at the Restoration.

"The pageants were abolished by order of the Corporation in 1678.

"'No circumstance,' says the old history from which we have already quoted, 'can evince the strange mutations to which things are liable, more than this place, which was originally a *chapel* dedicated to *St. Nicholas*, and devoted to *religion;* afterwards a *common hall* devoted to *justice;* next a *warehouse* devoted to *trade;* and now a *playhouse* devoted to *amusement.*'

"The present writer has to note another change : the 'playhouse' has become a MUSIC HALL, handsome and commodious.

"Previous to the Roman conquests, the Britons were accustomed to celebrate the rites of Druidism; but as it was the custom of the Romans to carry into the lands they conquered not only their civil polity, but also their religion, the gods of the Pantheon became consequently the gods of our ancestors. Near the existing memorials of Druidical superstition there arose the majestic fanes of a more polished mythology. At Bath there is said to have been a temple dedicated to Minerva, while on the site now occupied by the splendid cathedral of St. Paul there was a temple to Diana. It appears, from a passage in King's 'Vale Royal,' there was a tradition generally accepted in his day, that on the present site of Chester Cathedral was a temple dedicated to Apollo, during the period that the city was inhabited by the Legionaries."

CHAPTER XVII.

HE foregoing chapters have been devoted to descriptions which I have thought would be more interesting to the general reader than anything I could write concerning my enterprise, or the success with which the company met. The last active operations of the troupe, thus far mentioned, were in London, from which city we departed for Brighton, the famous English watering-place.

In 1750, this city was only a small fishing-village, and owes its rise, in the first instance, to being the chosen residence of George IV. when Prince of Wales. It is in the county of Sussex, on the English channel, fifty miles south of London, and is built between and on the two slopes of a range of chalk-hills. It has a sea-front of three miles in length, with a pavement and carriage-road of great width, flanked by houses of a superior class, rendering it, undoubtedly, the finest marine promenade in the kingdom.

The climate of Brighton is very salubrious, which has rendered it a famous place for the education of the English youths, upwards of two hundred and fifty schools being established there.

It has public charitable, scientific, and literary societies; and although there are no public buildings of great beauty, the Royal Pavilion, erected by George IV. deserves especial mention, from its unique and fantastic appearance. In the banqueting hall of this edifice we gave concerts. This was sixty feet long by forty-two wide, and forty-five high. Every room in the building is gorgeously decorated in Eastern style. The whole suite, at the time of our visit, was used for balls, assemblies, etc. For a dressing-room, we occupied what was once the sleeping-apartment of King George. The palace was purchased by Queen Victoria; but she did not like Brighton as a watering-place. The Pavilion was, at the time of which I write, owned by the town of Brighton.

The royal stabling, also owned by the town, is one of the most magnificent piles ever erected for such a purpose in Europe. It has the form of an octagon without, and a circle within, and is lighted by a glazed dome, of a diameter only twenty feet less than that of the dome of St. Paul's Cathedral, London.

The old parish church, which stands on the sun
mit of a hill, was formerly used as a sea beaco
There are now about forty churches in Brighton.

⸜The sea-wall, which protects, the whole easte
part of the town, is sixty feet in height, and has
terrace raised fifteen feet from the beach.

There is a chalybeate spring near the town, ai
the German waters are successfully imitated at t
Spa.

Every one who has had experience with waterin
places can sympathize with me when I inform thei
that Brighton, in the matter of high prices, w
no exception to the general rule in this countr
We were obliged to pay quite as much for what i
did not have as for what we did; and, before
ventured to use a clean towel, while in the act (
ablution, I looked cautiously about, to see if sor
one was not standing ready to demand a penny
two as the price of my extravagance.

As a result of my experience, I found th
Brighton was, indeed, an unprofitable field of spe
ulation; the "profits" of the concerts really n
equalling the sum expended by the troupe for t
necessaries of life, which, in that climate, rank
in price with the luxuries of existence.

Although there were many other places in En
land which I desired to visit, I saw that to attem
to continue the tour would be very unwise; an

consequently, proposed to the troupe that we again turn our faces towards Liverpool, and, as soon as expedient, sail for America.

This proposition did not meet with the favor which I had anticipated; and after hearing a free expression of opinion, found, for the first time in my life, that the convictions of Father Kemp and his "Old Folks" were directly opposed. The singers were willing to remain, and I was determined not to stay. Consequently I left them at Brighton; and, after a liberal share of inconveniences generally suffered by travellers, again arrived in good old Boston, and took the first train for Reading.

The fact of my arrival home without the troupe led to inquiry, and the facts in the case were readily furnished to those who, as I thought, had a right to know. Like some of my previous performances, this soon "got into the papers," and a correspondent of the "Middlesex Journal" wrote an article, to which I replied in the following letter, which gives, in a condensed form, the main facts of the English tour, some of which have not before been mentioned in this volume, —

"As it has already been announced in your journal that some account of my European adventure should be given to your readers this week, I will venture to send you a brief report of this novel undertaking

from the commencment up to the time I left
company in the city of Brighton, England, hop
thereby to correct the impressions made by
curiously formed stories which in these hard tin
can be so cheaply manufactured and peddled
from house to house and shop to shop.

"When the subject of going to Europe ʼ
brought before the class last December, I asl
each member of my company, 'Are you willing to
on the 9th of January, '61, and pay your own fa
fifty dollars each, and take the second cabin?' *ʌ*
with a few exceptions, were ready, and promised
go at that time, and also to pay in one-half, twen
five dollars each, when the passage was secur
and the remainder about six days before sailin
which was promptly done by all except six or se·
who had not the means, but were supplied by r
self and Mr. Jarrett, my agent, he paying one-h
and I the other, for those who could not meet
demand themselves.

"The 9th of January came, a fine, clear, c
morning; and as the hour for sailing drew n·
(10 A. M.), the 'Old Folks,' with groups
friends and relations, crowded the cabin and de
of the noble steamship CANADA, to bid adieu to ʄ
singular assemblage of vocal and instrume:
artists who were doting upon the honor of being

*

first exportation of the kind to the shores of 'Noble Old England.'

"The hour of sailing arrived, the bells rang, word was given to let go the rope, and soon her ponderous wheels were in motion, bearing us rapidly out in mid ocean, which soon brought us in contact with heavy seas and fierce winds, which continued their familiar games with us day and night until we had safely landed on terra firma in the city of Liverpool, landing in due time to commence a ten days' engagement at St. George's Hall. Our opening night, being January 23d, drew together a large assembly and a good paying house, with which we were nightly favored during our stay in that city, clearing over all expenses about five hundred dollars. From Liverpool we went direct to London, a distance of two hundred and ten miles, and commenced a series of about forty concerts on the night of February 11th, at St. James' Hall, the avails of which (to the everlasting disappointment of the 'Old Folks') replenished our treasury with the little sum amounting to twelve pounds ten shillings only. The next night we took in that great city eleven pounds; on the third night we took thirteen pounds; on the fourth night we took ten pounds; the fifth, seven pounds; on the sixth day, afternoon and evening, thirty-three pounds; our average receipts for the five weeks being about twelve pounds per night, which, with the afternoon concerts at the hall and Crystal Palace, amounted to little over twenty pounds per day.

"But this sum was hardly sufficient to pay advertising bills in thirty papers, and other necessary charges, which in England are always much larger than similar bills in America.

"From London we went to Brighton, a city of about eighty thousand inhabitants; and here our success was about the same as in London, receiving from eight to fifteen pounds per night. On the whole we had, up to the time I left, made no money, our daily expenses quite balancing the receipts.

"Finding we were not likely to succeed in making anything over expenses, I advised that we turn back and travel towards Liverpool, instead of taking another direction, that we could more easily find our way to the United States. But a majority of the company said '*No;* we are out here for a good time, and if we can get our board we are satisfied.' In view of this state of feeling, I told them I could not and should not stay there.

"But still I am often asked why I left the company, why I came home so soon, and why I did not stay one or two years, as I intimated when I left America? I would say that I left for several reasons: First, we were making no money, and had no prospect of doing better; second, I left because I did not like the expensive way our business was managed.

I left because I was ready to go home, and they were willing to have me. And again, I left because I had accomplished the great object of my visit to that country, which was (as my agent had published throughout England) for *pleasure, observation,* and *study.*

" I have experienced the *pleasure* of transporting the largest concert company to England that had ever crossed the Atlantic, and the exquisite *pleasure* of bringing back the smallest one. I had had the *pleasure* of knowing how popular my ' Old Folks'' company was in that country, and I had the *pleasure* of reading in the daily journals all the scathing things that could be said about the singing of good old American music. I had the *pleasure* of going to England, and now have had the *pleasure* of coming back again as quick as I went. So much for the pleasure of the trip. Our next object was *observation.* Having had the *pleasure* to my fill, I soon began to observe that it didn't pay. Ah, no, it did not pay at all ! I then took another *observation,* and found the soles of my boots thin, my wallet light, and growing worse and worse. I then took the third and last *observation,* which satisfied me fully that the English thought but little of the American people, or their music, especially the kind of music we sang ; that it would be a long while before we could gain a paying popularity among them. This led my attention to the third and last object of our European tour, which was *study*. This engrossed my whole thoughts. I *studied* night and day, having had the *pleasure* and the *observation*. I was in a deep *study* to know how I could best get out of the sad fix I was well into. My *study* was, how shall I get home. I determined at once to leave with what little cash I had left.

"Therefore, under these circumstances, I left the troupe at Brighton, as stated by your correspondent of last week, and would advise all who wish for similar experiences, to take over a sewing, printing, or cracker-machine, or some other American novelty in the shape of an 'Old Folks'' concert company, and I will guarantee all the pleasure, observation, and study one's heart or head can hold.   "R. KEMP."

The "Old Folks" did not remain long in England after my departure, and in the course of a few months all had returned home, much wiser, in many respects, than when they left America.

I was not content to remain idle in musical matters, and the "Old Folks" were again organized for a new campaign, which was begun by entertainments under the style of "Monday Popular Concerts," and were given in the Tremont Temple, Boston, before audiences which crammed the house, filled the stairways and vestibules, and crowded the sidewalk in front. On these occasions we had the assistance of the Boston Brigade Band, and the entertainments proved as popular as those given many years before.

I shall never forget the pleasing emotions experienced by me when I again rapped with my baton before hosts of friends in the Temple, raised it aloft, and said to the company, "All please sound;" and I do not believe the "sound" was ever so grateful to my ears as on that occasion.

These concerts were many times repeated, both at the Tremont Temple and in many other halls in various parts of the country occupied by the troupe in previous years, a simple mention of which will here suffice, as the reader is, doubtless, by this time heartily tired of reading descriptions of these occasions. Everywhere we went the same cordial greeting awaited us, and the fact that the peculiarities of the entertainments had not been forgotten was most clearly illustrated at one of these latter series. It had always been my custom to invite the congregation to join with us when we sang "Coronation." But I generally took occasion to remark, after it was finished, that I noticed "two or three in the audience" who did not sing, and proposed that "we all try it again." (About one in a dozen of the spectators joined us, really.) The good old tune was

generally given several times before *all* sung. On
the evening above referred to (in a town where the
congregation had at former concerts "joined" us six
or eight times), I made the same proposition again,
when a sharp voice was heard in the back part of
the hall : " *You can't come that 'ere in this town
again, old fellow; you tried it on us ten years ago.*"
I did not insist on the repetition, and we had, instead, roars of laughter for several minutes.

Two very pleasant occasions among my later concerts were enjoyed through the instrumentality of Dr.
S. O. Richardson, of South Reading, who proposed
that I should give entertainments for the children
of the public schools in Reading, he bearing all the
expenses, which his liberality made more than were
really necessary.   If his "Sherry Wine Bitters"
prove to be of as much benefit to the general public
as these concerts were to the juveniles, then it cannot be denied that he is doing much good.   The
doctor sat on the platform with the "Old Folks,"
but in the amount of pleasure experienced I think
he was one of the children.

Mrs. Emma J. Nichols was my leading soprano
for eight years, her husband accompanying the
troupe as treasurer. She was a great favorite wherever she appeared, and has received many notices
from the press, of which any vocalist might well
feel proud.   She did not simply sing with the cho-

rus, but her favorite songs were often interspersed throughout the programme. It is pleasant to record her great success; but in doing so I do not wish to ignore the worth of others who have participated with me in the unique entertainments known as "Old Folks' Concerts."

All who have been connected with me have my heartfelt thanks. No company, I believe, ever were so long together with less disagreements and wrangles. They were all ladies and gentlemen, and never lost consciousness of the fact under the most trying and perplexing circumstances.

Gentle reader, — you have perused this volume, and I know opinion as to its merits will be somewhat divided. But one thing is certain, — if "variety is the spice of life," the book has some of this grateful seasoning in its pages. You have followed me from Cape Cod, through a greater portion of the Northern, Middle, and Western States, across the Atlantic, and back again to America, which I propose never again to leave, with an "Old Folks' Concert Troupe." There is but one thing more you can do, — follow me to No. 794 Washington St., Boston, and let me sell you a pair of boots. If you have been bored in looking over the preceding pages, I will make amends by a reduction on my regular, but low, price per pair. I have taken much

13

pleasure in giving "Old Folks' concerts," for I
thought I was pleasing both old and young; this
conviction controls my present occupation, and as
there is nothing so desirable as a good "understand-
ing" with all parties, my shelves contain everything
from the copper-toed shoe for the creeping picca-
niny, to the number twelve of the full-grown man.
I hope I am not sordid in these expressions. I
always had a great liking for the public, and it was
never stronger than now. The admission to my
hall is free, and all are cordially invited to come.

Should I ever again appear in the capacity of conductor of an "Old Folks' Concert," do not refuse to
patronize me because I rank among those who have
written autobiographies; of which class, I fear, the
public have some reason to feel shy.

Again, do not stay away because you think I have
grown rich by becoming an author. I concede,
beforehand, that the literary part of my career is a
failure, and anticipate more pecuniary embarrass-
ment from having been rash enough to pen my
experiences, and causing them to be bound in book
form, than from any other act of my life.

If you have any credit to give me, let it be reserved for what you are yet to read. If a man is to
become a lawyer, he studies law; if a physician, he
studies medicine; if a minister, he studies theol-
ogy; if an editor, he practises with the pen and

pistol; and if a musical director, he becomes proficient in the arts of music.

This latter statement has been completely upset by my career; for, although I have swung my baton before a large choir in upwards of six thousand concerts, my word upon it, I NEVER KNEW A NOTE OF MUSIC, AND CANNOT DISTINGUISH A "MINIM" FROM A "DEMISEMIQUAVER." I flatter myself, however, that I can beat time with the most accomplished impressario.

SACRED AND SECULAR PIECES

SUNG BY

FATHER KEMP'S OLD FOLKS.

SACRED SELECTIONS.

STRIKE THE CYMBAL.

Strike the cymbal, roll the tymbal,
    Let the trump of triumph sound;
Powerful slinging, headlong bringing,
    Proud Goliath to the ground.
From the river, rejecting quiver,
    Judah's hero takes the stone;
Spread your banners,
    Shout hosanna, battle is the Lord's alone.

See, advances, with songs and dances,
All the band of Israel's daughters;
Catch the sound, ye hills and waters;
God of thunder! rend asunder
    All the power Philistia boasts.
What are nations? what their stations?
    Israel's God is Lord of hosts.

What are haughty monarchs now?
Lo, before Jehovah bow;
Pride of princes, strength of kings,
To the dust Jehovah brings;
Praise him, exulting nations, praise;
Hosanna.

THE HILL OF SION.

The hill of Sion yields
   A thousand sacred sweets,
Before we reach the heavenly fields,
   Or walk the golden streets.
Then let our songs abound,
   And every tear be dry;
We're marching through Immanuel's ground,
   To fairer worlds on high.

HOW LONG, DEAR SAVIOUR.

How long, dear Saviour, oh, how long
   Shall this bright hour delay;
Fly swifter round, ye wheels of time,
   And bring the welcome day.

THE DYING CHRISTIAN.

Vital spark of heavenly flame,
Quit, oh quit, this mortal frame!
Trembling, hoping, lingering, flying!
Oh, the pain, the bliss of dying!

Cease, fond nature, cease thy strife,
And let me languish into life!
Hark! they whisper, angels say, —
"Sister spirit, come away!"

What is this absorbs me quite,
Steals my senses, shuts my sight,
Drowns my spirit, draws my breath?
Tell me, my soul, can this be death?

The world recedes, it disappears;
Heaven opens on my eyes!
My ears with sounds seraphic ring!
Lend, lend your wings! I mount, I fly,
O grave, where is thy victory?
O death, where is thy sting?

ETERNAL POWER.

Eternal power, whose high abode
Becomes the grandeur of a God;
Infinite lengths, beyond the bounds
Where stars revolve their little rounds.

COME, MY BELOVED.

Come, my beloved, haste away,
Cut short the hours of thy delay;
Fly, like youthful hart or roe,
Over the hills where spices grow.

WHILE SHEPHERDS WATCHED.

While shepherds watched their flocks by night,
  All seated on the ground,
The angel of the Lord came down,
  And glory shone around.

BEFORE JEHOVAH'S AWFUL THRONE.

Before Jehovah's awful throne,
   Ye nations, bow with sacred joy;
Know that the Lord is God alone;
   He can create, and he destroy.

His sovereign power, without our aid,
   Made us of clay, and formed us men;
And when, like wandering sheep, we strayed,
   He brought us to his fold again.

We'll crowd Thy gates with thankful songs,
   High as the heaven our voices raise;
And earth, with her ten thousand tongues,
   Shall fill Thy courts with sounding praise.

Wide as the world is Thy command,
   Vast as eternity Thy love;
Firm as a rock Thy truth shall stand,
   When rolling years shall cease to move.

THE LORD IS RISEN.

The Lord is risen indeed,
   Hallelujah.
Now is Christ risen from the dead,
And become the first fruits of them that slept.
   Hallelujah.
And did he rise, did he rise?
   Hallelujah.
Hear, O ye nations,
Hear it, O ye dead:
He rose, he rose, he rose,
He burst the bars of death,
And triumphed o'er the grave.

Then, then, then I rose,
Then first humanity triumphant passed the crystal
    ports of light,
And seized eternal youth.
Man, all immortal, hail! hail!
Heaven all lavish of strange gifts to man,
Thine all the glory, man's the boundless bliss.

———◦◦◦———

COME, SHED ABROAD.

Come, shed abroad a Saviour's love,
    And that shall kindle ours,
Come, Holy Spirit, heavenly dove,
    With all thy quickening powers.

———◦◦◦———

METHINKS I SEE A HEAVENLY HOST.

Methinks I see a heavenly host
    Of angels on the wing;
Methinks I hear their cheerful notes,
    So merrily they sing, —

" Let all your fears be banished hence;
    Glad tidings we proclaim,
For there's a Saviour born to-day,
    And Jesus is his name."

———◦◦◦———

HOW VAIN ARE ALL THINGS.

How vain are all things here below!
    How false and yet how fair!
Each pleasure hath its poison too,
    And every sweet a snare,
Each pleasure hath its poison too,
    And every sweet a snare.

ALL HAIL! THE POWER OF JESUS' NAME.

All hail! the power of Jesus' name;
    Let angels prostrate fall;
Bring forth the royal diadem,
    And crown him Lord of all,
Bring forth the royal diadem,
    And crown him Lord of all,

Let every kindred, every tribe,
    On this terrestrial ball,
To him all majesty ascribe,
    And crown him Lord of all,
To him all majesty ascribe,
    And crown him Lord of all.

———

DAVID'S LAMENTATION.

David the king was grieved and moved,
He went to his chamber, and wept!
Would to God I had died, O my son,
O Absalom, my son, my son!

———

SONS OF ZION.

Sons of Zion, come before him,
Bring the cymbal, bring the harp
High in glory, lo! he's seated,
See the King, he sits in state.

THE WORKS OF GLORY.

The works of glory, mighty Lord,
  That rule the boist'rous sea,
The sons of courage shall record,
  Who tempt that dangerous way.

At Thy command the winds arise,
  And swell the tow'ring waves;
The men, astonished, mount the skies,
  And sink in gaping graves.

EARLY, MY GOD.

Early, my God, without delay,
  I haste to seek Thy face;
My thirsty spirit faints away,
  Without Thy cheering grace:

So pilgrims on the scorching sand,
  Beneath a burning sky,
Long for a cooling stream at hand, —
  And they must drink or die.

O THOU, TO WHOM ALL CREATURES BOW.

O Thou, to whom all creatures bow,
  Within this earthly frame,
Through all the world how great art Thou!
  How glorious is Thy name!

SPARE US, O LORD!

Spare us, O Lord! aloud we cry,
  Nor let our sun go down at noon;
Thy years are one eternal day,
  And must Thy children die so soon?

PRAISE GOD FROM WHOM.

Praise God from whom all blessings flow;
Praise him, all creatures here below;
Praise him, above, ye heavenly host,
Praise Father, Son, and Holy Ghost.

MY SOUL, THY GREAT CREATOR PRAISE.

My soul, Thy great Creator praise,
When clothed in his celestial rays,
He in full majesty appears,
And like a robe his glory wears.

NOW CAN MY SOUL.

Now can my soul in God rejoice;
I feel my Saviour's cheering voice;
My heart awakes to sing his praise,
And longs to join immortal lays.

Hold me, O Jesus, in thine arms,
And cheer me with immortal charms,
Till I awake in realms above,
Forever to enjoy Thy love.

BEHOLD THE MORNING SUN.

Behold the morning sun
 Begins his glorious way;
His beams through all the nations run,
 And life and light convey.

But where the gospel comes,
 It spreads diviner light,
It calls dead sinners from their tombs,
 And gives the blind their sight.

'TIS BY THY STRENGTH.

'Tis by Thy strength the mountains stand,
 God of eternal power;
The sea grows calm at Thy command,
 And tempests cease to roar.

THE LORD DESCENDED.

The Lord descended from above,
 And bowed the heavens most high;
And underneath his feet he cast
 The darkness of the sky.

On cherub and on cherubim
 Full royally he rode;
And on the wings of mighty wind
 Came flying all abroad.

THE LORD IS OUR SHEPHERD.

The Lord is our shepherd, our guardian and guide,
Whatever we want, he will kindly provide;
To sheep of his pasture his mercies abound,
His care and protection his flock will surround.

SOUND THE LOUD TIMBREL.

Sound the loud timbrel o'er Egypt's dark sea;
Jehovah has triumphed; his people are free;
Sing, for the pride of the tyrant is broken;
　His chariots, his horsemen all splendid and brave;
How vain was their boasting! the Lord hath but spoken,
　And chariots and horsemen are sunk in the wave.

Praise to the Conqueror; praise to the Lord;
His word was our arrow; his breath was our sword;
Who shall return to tell Egypt the story
　Of those she sent forth in the hour of her pride?
The Lord hath looked out from his pillar of glory,
　And all her brave thousands are dashed in the tide.

FROM ZION'S SACRED MOUNTAIN.

See, from Zion's sacred mountain,
　Streams of living water flow!
God has opened there a fountain—
　This supplies the plain below.
They are blessèd, they are blessèd,
　Who its sovereign virtue know.

SAVIOUR, VISIT THY PLANTATION.

Saviour, visit thy plantation;
  Grant us, Lord, a gracious rain;
All will come to desolation,
  Unless thou return again.
Turn to the Lord and seek redemption,
  Sound the praise of his dear name;
Glory, honor, and salvation,
  Christ, the Lord, is come to reign.

Keep no longer at a distance,
  Shine upon us from on high;
Lest, for want of thine assistance,
  Every plant will droop and die;
    Turn to the Lord, etc.

JEHOVAH'S PRAISE.

Jehovah's praise, in high immortal strains,
Resound, ye heavens, through all your blissful plains.

TREBLE SOLO — ANDANTE.

His glorious power, O radiant sun, display,
Far as thy vital beams diffuse the day;
Thou silver moon, arrayed in softer lights,
Recount his wonders to the listening nights;
Let all thy glittering train attendant wait,
And every star his Maker's name repeat.

ALLEGRO.

His glorious power, etc.

DUET — ALLEGRETTO.

Ye glorious angels tune the raptured lay
Through the fair mansions of eternal day;

His praise, let all the shining ranks proclaim,
And teach the distant worlds your Maker's name.

CHORUS — ALLEGRO MOTTO.

Bright with the splendor of his dazzling rays,
Exalted realms of joy reflect his praise.

ROCKED IN THE CRADLE.

Music by J. P. Knight.

Rocked in the cradle of the deep,
I lay me down in peace to sleep;
Secure I rest upon the wave,
For thou, O Lord! hast power to save.
I know thou wilt not slight my call,
For thou dost mark the sparrow's fall!
And calm and peaceful is my sleep,
Rocked in the cradle of the deep.

And such the trust that still were mine,
Though stormy winds swept o'er the brine;
Or, though the tempest's fury breath,
Roused me from sleep to wreck or death;
In ocean cave still safe with Thee,
The germ of immortality.
 And calm, etc.

From the Haymakers.

HOW GOOD IS THE GIVER.

QUINTETTE.

How good is he, the Giver,
Whose mercies fail us never,
Whose bounty large is ever
Loving and free.

From him, the bright sun shineth,
Shineth the bright sun, glorious light,
And soft as eve declineth,
Softly declineth, bringing the night.

His power the season changeth,
Summer and Winter, Autumn and Spring,
And each, his praise proclaimeth,
Ever the bountiful Lord and King.

For everything he careth,
His notice nothing spareth, —
Not e'en the sparrow falleth
Without his kind regard.

And here his love hath brought us,
His goodness here hath taught us
That we with one accord,
May praise the Lord;

Yet learn we a lesson from the falling grass, —
In the morning it flourisheth and groweth up,
In the evening it is cut down and withereth;
So in a day our life may be ended;

When that time shall come, may we be gathered into the
garner of the Most High.
Praise the Lord.

———◦◦———

EXHORTATION.

Now, in the heat of youthful blood,
Remember your Creator, God,
Behold the months come hast'ning on,
When you shall say my joys are gone.

14

MILFORD.

If angels sung a Saviour's birth
On that auspicious morn,
We well may imitate their mirth,
Now He again is born.

LYNNFIELD.

My God, permit me not to be
A stranger to myself and thee!
Amidst ten thousand thoughts I rove,
Forgetful of my highest love.
Why should my passions mix with earth,
And thus debase my heavenly birth?
Why should I cleave to things below,
And let my God, my Saviour go?

Call me away from flesh and sense;
One sov'reign word can call me thence;
I would obey the voice divine,
And all inferior joys resign.
Be earth with all her scenes withdrawn,
Let noise and vanity be gone;
In secret silence of the mind,
My heav'n, my heav'n, my heav'n and there, my God, I find.

TOPSFIELD.

Lo! what an entertaining sight
  Are brethren who agree;
Whose hands with cheerful hearts unite,
  In bonds of piety;
When streams of love from Christ the spring,
  Descend to ev'ry soul,
And heav'nly peace, with balmy wing,
  Shades and bedews the whole.

HALLOWELL.

As on some lonely building's top
   The sparrow tells her moan,
Far from the tents of joy and hope,
   I sit and grieve alone.

SOLITUDE.

My refuge is the God of love;
   My foes insult and cry,
Fly like a tim'rous, trembling dove,
   To distant mountains fly.

Since I have placed my trust in God,
   A refuge always nigh,
Why should I, like a tim'rous bird
   To distant mountains fly?

DELIGHT.

No burning heats by day,
   Nor blasts of evening air,
Shall take my health away,
   If God be with me there.
Thou art my sun,
   And thou my shade,
To guard my head
   By night or noon.

OH, WHERE SHALL REST BE FOUND?

Oh, where shall rest be found, —
  Rest for the weary soul?
'Twere vain the ocean-depths to sound,
  Or pierce to either pole.

The world can never give
  The bliss for which we sigh:
'Tis not the whole of life to live,
  Nor all of death to die.

Beyond this vale of tears,
  There is a life above,
Unmeasured by the flight of years;
  And all that life is love.

Here would we end our quest:
  Alone are found in thee
The life of perfect love, — the rest
  Of immortality.

OH CEASE, MY WANDERING SOUL.

Oh cease, my wandering soul,
  On restless wing to roam!
All this wide world, to either pole,
  Has not for thee a home.

Behold the ark of God!
  Behold the open door!
Oh, haste to gain that dear abode,
  And rove, my soul, no more!

There, safe thou shalt abide;
  There, sweet shall be thy rest;
And every longing satisfied,
  With full salvation blest.

PARADISE.

Now to the shining realms above
  I stretch my hands and glance my eyes;
Oh for the pinions of the dove
  To bear me to the upper skies;
There from the bosom of my God
  Oceans of endless pleasure roll;
There would I fix my last abode,
  And drown the sorrows of my soul.

MONTAGUE.

Ye sons of men, with joy record
The various wonders of the Lord,
And let his power and goodness sound
Through all your tribes the world around.
Let the high heavens your songs invite, —
Those spacious fields of brilliant light,
Where sun, and moon, and planets roll,
And stars that glow from pole to pole.

ARCHDALE.

When God revealed his gracious name,
  And changed my mournful state,
My rapture seemed a pleasing dream,
  Thy grace appeared so great;
The world beheld the glorious change,
  And did thy hand confess;
My tongue broke out in unknown strains,
  And sung surprising grace.

BUCKFIELD.

When strangers stand and hear me tell
What beauties in my Saviour dwell,
Where he is gone they fain would know,
That they may seek and love him too.

WHY DO WE MOURN.

Why do we mourn departing friends,
  Or shake at death's alarms?
'Tis but the voice that Jesus sends
  To call them to his arms.

NEW JERUSALEM.

From the third heaven, where God resides,
  That holy, happy place,
The New Jerusalem comes down,
  Adorned with shining grace.

LORD, DISMISS US.

Lord, dismiss us with thy blessing;
  Bid us all depart in peace;
Still on gospel manna feeding,
  Pure, seraphic love increase.
Fill each breast with consolation;
  Up to thee our hearts we'll raise,
Till we reach that blissful station,
  Where we'll give thee nobler praise,
And sing hallelujah, to God and the Lamb.

SECULAR SELECTIONS.

YANKEE'S RETURN FROM CAMP.

Father and I went down to camp,
 Along with Captain Gooding,
And there we see the men and boys,
 As thick as hasty pudding.
  Yankee doodle, keep it up,
  Yankee doodle dandy,
  Beneath the fig-tree and the vine,
  Sing Yankee doodle dandy.

And there we see a swamping gun,
 Large as a log of maple,
Upon a deuced little cart,
 A load for father's cattle.
  Yankee doodle, etc.

And every time they shoot it off,
 It takes a horn of powder;
It makes a noise like father's gun,
 Except a nation louder.
  Yankee doodle, etc.

I went as nigh to one myself
 As Siah's underpinning,
And father went as nigh again, —
 I thought the deuce was in him.
  Yankee doodle, etc.

Cousin Simon grew so bold,
   I thought he would have cocked it;
It scared me so, I streaked it off,
   And hung to father's pocket.
     Yankee doodle, etc.

Captain Davis had a gun,
   He kind of clapped his hand on't,
And stuck a crooked stabbing-iron
   Upon the little end on't.
     Yankee doodle, etc.

And there I see a pumpkin-shell
   As big as mother's basin,
And every time they touched it off,
   They scampered like the nation.
     Yankee doodle, etc.

I see a little barrel, too,
   The heads were made of leather;
They knocked on it with little clubs,
   And called the folks together.
     Yankee doodle, etc.

And there was Captain Washington,
   And gentlefolks about him;
They say he's grown so tarnal proud,
   He will not ride without 'em.
     Yankee doodle, etc.

He got him on his meeting clothes,
   Upon a slapping stallion,
He set the world along in rows,
   In hundreds and in millions.
     Yankee doodle, etc.

I see another snarl of men,
   A-digging graves, they told me,
So tarnal long, so tarnal deep,
   They 'tended they should hold me.
     Yankee doodle, etc.

It scared me so I scampered off,
Nor stopped, as I remember,
Nor turned about till I got home,
Locked up in mother's chamber.
Yankee doodle, etc.

Yankee doodle, keep it up,
Yankee doodle dandy,
Beneath the fig-tree and the vine,
Sing Yankee doodle dandy.
Yankee doodle, etc.

THE MANOLA.

Music composed by Paul Henrion.

Of Aragon, of bright Castilla
Thou, called most fair, in cot or villa,
Come, join us here; 'neath thy mantilla,
　Why linger thus, hiding thy face?
Dost thou not hear sweet music sounding?
In lively dance light feet are bounding,
Gay young Manolas with glance confounding,
　Sing as they dance, ever with grace.
Come, then, Juanita, come with me, dearest;
　Quick to the Prado! each one's in place,
Waiting to crown thee, brightest and fairest,
　Queen of the Jota Aragonaise;
Ah! ah! ah! ah! Waiting to crown thee
Brightest and fairest
　Queen of the Jota Aragonaise.

Dost thou not know what is occurring? —
How Grenada all Spain is stirring,
Sending this way beauties alluring,
　All their most fair, their dance to grace.

Come, then, with me, night is advancing,
Crowds from Madrid gayly are prancing
Out to behold Spain's beauties dancing.
    None of them all can fill thy place.
        Come, then, Juanita, etc.

But all is hushed in thy loved dwelling;
Only the breeze, sobbing and swelling,
Wails through the trees, their dead leaves **impelling.**
    All else is still; I watch and sigh:
When a sweet voice, soft and endearing,
Speaks from within accents so cheering;
Soon the fair maiden gayly appearing,
    Answers my call, "Yes, here am I."
Place on the Prado, quickly obtaineth
    Fair Juanita, model of grace;
Charming Manola, ever remaineth
    Queen of the Jota Aragonaise.
        Come, then, Juanita, etc.

——◆——

THE CAPTAIN.

As they marched through the town, with their **banners so gay,**
I ran to the window to hear the band play;
I peeped through the blind very cautiously then,
Lest the neighbors should say I was looking at the men.
Oh! I heard the drums beat and the music so sweet;
But my eyes at the time caught a much greater treat:
The troop was the finest I ever did see,
And the captain with his whiskers took a sly glance at me

When we met at the ball I of course thought 'twas right
To pretend that we never had met before that night;
But he knew me at once, I could see by his glance,
And I hung down my head when he asked me to dance.
Oh, he sat by my side at the end of the set,
And the **sweet** words he spoke I shall never forget;

For my heart was enlisted and could not get free,
As the captain with his whiskers took a sly glance at me.

But he marched from the town and I see him no more,
Yet I think of him oft, and the whiskers he wore;
I dream all the night and I talk all the day
Of the love of a captain who has gone far away;
I remember, with superabundant delight,
When we met in the street, and we danced all the night,
And keep in my mind how my heart jumped with glee
As the captain with his whiskers took a sly glance at me.

ODE ON SCIENCE.

Old American Ode.

The morning sun shines from the east,
And spreads his glories to the west;
All nations with his beams are blest,
Where'er his radiant light appears.
So Science spreads her lucid ray
O'er lands that long in darkness lay;
She visits fair Columbia,
And sets her sons among the stars.

Fair Freedom, her attendant, waits
To bless the portals of her gates;
To crown the young and rising states
With laurels of immortal day.
No daring foe, with impious hand,
Shall e'er invade our heaven-blest land;
United in a glorious band,
We'll shout, "Long live America!"

WHAT'S A' THE STEER KIMMER?

What's a' the steer, kimmer? what's a' the steer?
Jamie is landed, and soon he will be here;
Go lace your bodice blue, lassie, lace your bodice blue,
Put on your Sunday claithes, and trim your cap anew,
For I'm right glad o' heart, kimmer, right glad o' heart,
I ha'e a bonny breast-knot, and for his sake I'll wear't;
Sin' Jamie is come hame we ha'e nae care to fear,
Bid the neighbors all come down and welcome Jamie here.

Where's Donald Tod, lassie? rin fetch him here,
Bid him bring his pipes, lassie, bid him tune them clear,
For we'll taste the barley mow, foot it to and fro;
Sin' Jamie is come hame we'll gie him hearty cheer.
And it's what's a' the steer kimmer? what's a' the steer?
Jamie is landed, and soon he will be here;
Bid Allen Ramsey rin, bid him kill a fatted deer,
Oh, the neighbors little ken how welcome Jamie's here.

WHEN THE QUIET MOON IS BEAMING.

Music by J. Schondorf.

When the quiet moon is beaming
　　Over streamlet, vale, and hill,
When the weary world lies dreaming,
　　All around so calm and still;
Then, my tuneful lyre retaking,
　　Oft I stray the woods among,
While my heart, its silence breaking,
　　Pours a flood of grief and song.

O'er the strings my tears are falling;
　　Ah! beloved, what'er I see,
All my vanished bliss recalling,
　　Speaks of thee, of only thee.

Now thou'rt gone, my buried treasure!
  Now the grass-green earth's thy tomb;
Nought remains of joy and pleasure,
  All is solitude and gloom.

Now, the glorious sun appearing,
  All night's shadows flee away;
Nature, wakening, warming, cheering,
  With the magic of his ray.
Now Hope whispers, cease to sorrow,
  Soon shall cease thy grief, thy pain;
Soon shall dawn a brighter morrow,
  When thou'lt meet thy love again.

THE TWILIGHT HOUR.

Composed by G. Bristow.

At twilight hour I love to steal,
  Unseen, unheard, when none are near,
To nurse the pensive pain I feel,
  And shed alone fond memory's tear.
At that loved hour sad things arise,
  Of friends by absence made more dear,
Fond cherished hopes, long-severed ties
  And blighted feeling cold and drear.

Then thought reverts to other days,
  Sweet tones arise, loved forms appear,
And memory tells of other lays,
  Breathed to fond friendship's listening ear.
Yet do I love the twilight hour,
  For thou a soothing balm canst bring,
And fancy's sweet and soothing power
  Blunts kindly, memory's poignant sting.

HOME OF MY HEART.

I breathe once more my native air,
   And hail each happy, happy scene,
That rises round me everywhere,
   As though I left but yester e'en.

Oh! how I love thee, Erin dear!
   When roaming on a foreign strand,
In fancy still my steps were here,
   Home of my heart, my native land.

I've found the hour so fondly sought,
   And weep; but these are joyous tears,
The rapture of a moment bought
   By long and weary absent years.
     Oh! how I love thee, etc.

WITHIN A MILE OF EDINBORO' TOWN.

'Twas within a mile of Edinboro' town,
   In the rosy time of the year;
Sweet flowers bloomed and the grass was down,
   And each shepherd wooed his dear.
Bonny Jocky, blithe and gay,
Kissed sweet Jenny making hay;
The lassie blushed, and frowning cried, no, no, it will not do,
I cannot, cannot, wonnot, wonnot, munnot buckle too.

Jocky was a wag that never would wed,
   Though long he had followed the lass;
Contented she earned and ate her own bread,
   And merrily turned up the grass.
Bonny Jocky, blithe and free,
Won her heart right merrily;
Yet still she blushed and frowning cried, no, no, it will not do,
I cannot, cannot, wonnot, wonnot, munnot buckle too.

But when he vowed he would make her his bride,
　Though his flocks and herds were not few,
She gave him her hand and a kiss beside,
　And vowed she'd forever be true.
Bonny Jocky blithe and free,
Won her heart right merrily ;
At church she no more frowning, cried, no, no, it will not do,
I cannot, cannot, wonnot, wonnot, munnot buckle too.

——◦◦◦——

MARSEILLAISE HYMN.

Ye sons of freedom, wake to glory;
　Hark ! hark ! what myriads bid you rise ;
Your children, wives, and grandsires hoary,
　Behold their tears, and hear their cries !
Shall lawless tyrants, mischief breeding
　With hireling host, a ruffian band,
　Affright and desolate the land,
While peace and liberty lie bleeding?
　　To arms, to arms, ye brave !
　　　The patriot sword unsheath ;
　　March on, all hearts resolved
　　　On liberty or death.

Oh, liberty ! can man resign thee,
　Once having felt thy glorious flame?
Can tyrants' bolts and bars confine thee,
　And thus thy noble spirit tame?
Too long our country wept, bewailing
　The blood-stained sword our conquerors wield;
　But freedom is our sword and shield,
And all their arts are unavailing.
　　　To arms, etc.

THE DEAREST SPOT OF EARTH TO ME IS HOME.

The dearest spot of earth to me
  Is home, sweet home!
The fairy land I long to see
  Is home, sweet home!
There, how charmed the sense of hearing,
There, where love is so endearing!
All the world is not so cheering
  As home, sweet home!

I've taught my heart the way to prize
  My home, sweet home!
I've learned to look with lover's eyes
  On home, sweet home!
There, where vows are truly plighted!
There, where hearts are so united!
All the world besides I've slighted
  For home, sweet home.

GOD SAVE THE QUEEN.

God save our gracious Queen;
Long live our noble Queen;
God save the Queen;
Send her victorious,
Happy and glorious,
Long to reign over us;
God save the Queen.

O Lord, our God, arise,
Scatter her enemies,
And make them fall;
Confound their politics,
Frustrate their knavish tricks,
On thee our hopes we fix;
Oh, save us all.

15

Thy choicest gifts in store,
On her be pleased to pour,
Long may she reign;
May she defend our land,
And ever give us cause
To sing with heart and voice,
God save the Queen.

———◆———

SONG OF THE OLD FOLKS.

Should auld acquaintance be forgot,
  And never brought to mind;
Should auld acquaintance be forgot,
  And songs of auld lang syne?
For auld lang syne we meet to-night,
  For auld lang syne;
To sing the songs our fathers sang
  In days of auld lang syne.

We've passed through many varied scenes,
  Since youth's unclouded day;
And friends and hopes and happy dreams
  Time's hand hath swept away.
And voices that once joined with ours,
  In days of auld lang syne,
Are silent now and blend no more
  In songs of auld lang syne.

Yet ever has the light of song
  Illumed our darkest hours,
And cheered us on life's toilsome way,
  And gemmed our path with flowers;
The sacred songs our fathers sang,
  Dear songs of auld lang syne;
The hallowed songs our fathers sang
  In days of auld lang syne.

Here we have met, here we may part,
  To meet on earth no more;
And we may never sing again
  The cherished songs of yore;
The sacred songs our fathers sang
  In days of auld lang syne;
We may not meet to sing again
  The songs of auld lang syne.

But when we've crossed the sea of life,
  And reached the heavenly shore,
We'll sing the songs our fathers sang,
  Transcending those of yore;
We'll meet to sing diviner strains
  Than those of auld lang syne;
Immortal songs of praise, unknown
  In days of auld lang syne.

———◦∘◦———

COMIN' THROUGH THE RYE.

If a body meet a body,
  Comin' through the rye;
If a body kiss a body,
  Need a body cry?

Ev'ry lassie has her laddie,
  None they say ha'e I,
Yet a' the lads they smile at me,
  When comin' through the rye.

Among the train, there is a swain,
  I dearly lo'e mysel';
And what's his name, or where's his hame,
  I dinna choose to tell.
        Ev'ry lassie, etc.

If a body meet a body,
  Comin' fra the town;
If a body meet a body,
  Need a body frown?
    Ev'ry lassie, etc.

KIDD'S LAMENT.

You captains bold and brave, hear my cries, hear my cries,
You captains bold and brave, hear my cries;
You captains brave and bold, though you seem uncontrolled,
Don't for the sake of gold, lose your souls, lose your souls,
Don't for the sake of gold lose your souls.

My name was Robert Kidd, when I sailed, when I sailed,
My name was Robert Kidd, God's laws I did forbid,
And so wickedly I did, when I sailed, when I sailed,
And so wickedly I did when I sailed.

My parents taught me well, when I sailed, when I sailed,
To shun the gates of hell, when I sailed,
I cursed my father dear, and her that did me bear,
And so wickedly did swear, when I sailed, when I sailed,
And so wickedly did swear, when I sailed.

I'd a Bible in my hand, when I sailed, when I sailed,
But I sunk it in the sand, when I sailed;
I made a solemn vow to God I would not bow,
Nor myself one prayer allow, when I sailed, when I sailed,
Nor myself one prayer allow, when I sailed.

I murdered William Moore, as I sailed, as I sailed,
And left him in his gore, as I sailed,
And being cruel still, my gunner I did kill,
And much precious blood did spill, as I sailed, as I sailed,
And much precious blood did spill, as I sailed.

I took three ships from France, when I sailed, when I sailed,
Likewise three more from Spain, when I sailed,
But fourteen more by three, they were too much for me;
I am conquered now, you see, and must die, and must die;
Farewell the raging sea, I must die.

To Newgate now I'm cast, and must die, and must die,
At Execution Dock I must die;
Come, all you young and old, you're welcome to my gold,
For by it I've lost my soul, and must die,
For by it I've lost my soul; fare you well.

HOME AGAIN.

Words and Music by M. S. Pike.

Home again, home again, from a foreign shore,
  And oh! it fills my soul with joy
To meet my friends once more.
  Here I dropped the parting tear,
To cross the ocean's foam;
  But now I'm once again with those
Who kindly greet me home.
      Home again, etc.

Happy hearts, happy hearts, with mine have laughed in glee,
  But oh! the friends I loved in youth
Seem happier to me;
  And if my guide should be the fate
Which bids me longer roam,
  But death alone can break the tie
That binds my heart to home.
      Home again, etc.

Music sweet, music soft, lingers round the place,
  And oh! I feel the childhood charm
That time cannot efface;
  Then give me but my homestead roof,

I'll ask no palace dower;
For I can live a happy life
With those I love at home.
Home again, etc.

MINNIE CLYDE.

Oh, long have I sung of sweet Kitty Clyde,
Who lived at the foot of the hill;
And though that sweet pretty bird has flown,
Another is living there still.
She's blythe and gay as the robins that sing
On the trees by the old mill-side;
And if ever I loved a girl in my life,
'Tis the charming sweet Minnie Clyde.
Oh, Minnie Clyde, she is my pride,
And sure I am no jester;
For if ever I loved a girl in my life,
'Tis Minnie, Kitty Clyde's sister.

I think her eyes are brighter than Kitty's;
The dimple in her chin is deeper, —
I would be imprisoned the rest of my life
With Minnie Clyde for my keeper;
In the festive throng she sings a sweet song,
With the lowly alike is she meek;
Her eyes are the windows of her soul,
Through which Minnie's heart would speak.
Oh, Minnie Clyde, she is my pride, etc

Oh, blest are the hearts that live in the cot
That stands at the foot of the hill;
Oh, sweet are the songs that echo in the glen,
By the murmur of the moss-covered mill;
The birds all chant their notes to Minnie,
The angels above have caressed her,
But you have the angels, and you have the birds,
And I'll have Kitty Clyde's sister.
Oh, Minnie Clyde, she is my pride, etc.

STAR-SPANGLED BANNER.

Oh, say, can you see by the dawn's early light,
  What so proudly we hailed at the twilight's last gleaming,
Whose broad stripes and bright stars through the perilous
    fight,
  O'er the ramparts we watched, were so gallantly streaming,
And the rocket's red·glare, the bombs bursting in air,
Gave proof through the night, that our flag was still there,
Oh, say, does the star-spangled banner yet wave
O'er the land of the free, and the home of the brave?

On the shore dimly seen through the mists of the deep,
  Where the foe's haughty hosts in dread silence reposes,
What is that which the breeze o'er the towering sweep,
  As it fitfully blows, half conceals, half discloses?
Now it catches the gleam of the morning's first beam,
In full glory reflected, now shines on the stream;
'Tis the star-spangled banner, oh, long may it wave
O'er the land of the free, and the home of the brave!

And where is that band who so vauntingly swore
  That the havoc of war, and the battle's confusion,
A home and a country should leave us no more?
  Their blood has washed out their foul footsteps' pollution.
No refuge could save the hireling and slave,
From the terror of flight, or the gloom of the grave;
And the star-spangled banner in triumph doth wave
O'er the land of the free and the home of the brave.

Oh, thus be it ever, when freemen shall stand
  Between their loved home and the war's desolation;
Blessed with victory and peace, may the heaven-rescued land
  Praise the power that has made and preserved us a nation.
Then conquer we must, when our cause it is just,
And this be our motto. "In God is our Trust;"
And the star-spangled banner in triumph shall wave
O'er the land of the free, and the home of the brave.

HAIL, COLUMBIA!

Hail, Columbia, happy land!
Hail, ye heroes, heaven-born band,
Who fought and bled in freedom's cause,
And when the storm of war was gone,
Enjoyed the peace your valor won.
Let independence be your boast,
Ever mindful what it cost;
Ever grateful for the prize,
Let its altar reach the skies.
   Firm, united let us be,
   Rallying round our liberty!
   As a band of brothers joined,
   Peace and safety we shall find.

Immortal patriots, rise once more!
Defend your rights, defend your shore;
Let no rude foe, with impious hand,
Invade the shrine, where sacred lies,
Of toil and blood, the well-earned prize;
While offering peace sincere and just,
In Heaven we place a manly trust —
That truth and justice may prevail,
And every scheme of bondage fail.
      Firm, united, etc.

Sound, sound the trump of fame,
Let Washington's great name
Ring through the world with loud applause!
Let every clime, to freedom dear,
Listen with a joyful ear;
With equal skill, with steady power,
He governs in the fearful hour
Of horrid war, or guides with ease
The happier time of honest peace.
      Firm, united, etc.

Behold the chief, who now commands,
Once more to serve his country, stands,
The rock on which the storm will beat!
But armed in virtue, firm and true,
His hopes are fixed on Heaven and you;
When hope was sinking in dismay,
When gloom obscured Columbia's day,
His steady mind, from changes free,
Resolved on death or liberty.
      Firm, united, etc.

HOME, SWEET HOME.

'Mid pleasures and palaces though we may roam, —
Be it ever so humble, there's no place like home;
A charm from the skies seems to hallow us there,
Which, seek through the world, is ne'er met elsewhere.
      Home, home, sweet, sweet home!
      Be it ever so humble, there's no place like home.

An exile from home, splendor dazzles in vain;
Oh! give me my lowly thatched cottage again;
The birds singing gayly, that came at my call, —
Oh! give me that peace of mind, dearer than all.
      Home, home, etc.

NOBLE ENGLAND!

Noble old England! happiest of lands;
A pattern to nations thy green isle still stands;
Freedom's proud banner flaunts in the skies,
Where shouts of victory ever shall rise.
United in heart, united in hand,
Blest as a nation, by sea and by land,
Throughout the world our motto shall be,
" Health to thy commerce, and friendship to thee!"

Brave are thy sons, thy daughters are fair;
Emblems of beauty and valor they are;
Foremost in war the suffering to cheer;
First in oppression the burden to share;
Round thy schools and thy laws, forever divine,
May the rose, and the thistle, and shamrock entwine;
Engraven in letters of gold still be seen,
"Health to Old England, long live the Queen!"

ROBIN RUFF.

ROBIN.

If I'd but a thousand a-year, Gaffer Greene,
What a man would I be,
And what sights would I see,
If I'd but a thousand a-year.
　　If I'd but, etc.

GAFFER GREENE.

The best wish you could have,
Take my word, Robin Ruff,
Would scarce find you in bread or in beer;
But be honest and true,
And say what would you do,
If you had but a thousand a-year, Robin Ruff?
　　If you had, etc.

ROBIN.

I'd do, I scarcely know what, Gaffer Greene,
I'd go, — faith I hardly know where;
But I'd scatter the chink,
And leave others to think,
If I had but a thousand a-year,
　　If I had, etc.

GAFFER GREENE.

But when you are aged and gray, Robin Ruff,
And the day of your death draweth near,
Say what, with your pains,
Would you do with your gains,
If you then had but a thousand a-year, Robin Ruff?
    If you had, etc.

ROBIN.

I scarcely can tell what you mean, Gaffer Greene,
Your questions are always so queer;
But as other folks die,
I suppose so must I.

GAFFER GREENE.

What, and give up your thousand a-year, Robin
    Ruff?
    What, and give, etc.
There's a place that is better than this, Robin Ruff,
And I hope in my heart you'll go there,
Where the poor man is as great,
Though he hath no estate,
Ay, as if he'd a thousand a-year, Robin Ruff,
    Ay, as if, etc.

WHO TREADS THE PATH OF DUTY.

Who treads the path of duty,
Nor shrinks when honor calls,
Deserves the smiles of beauty,
Nor e'er inglorious falls;
His steps the great Osiris leads,
By gentle paths to gentle deeds,
And, with glad welcome, greets him here,
A pilgrim to a brighter sphere.

Who, in their hearts would cherish,
Or rage, or colder hate,
Would see another perish,
Or triumph o'er his fate;
Not such are found within these walls;
Here the soft tear of pity falls,
Each other's failings all forgive,
And all in peace and concord live.

EVE'S LAMENTATION.

Composed by King.

Must I leave thee, Paradise?
Must I leave thee, leave thee, native soil;
These happy walks, these walks and shades?
Oh, flowers! that never will in other climate grow,
Who now shall rear ye to the sun?
From thee, from thee, how can I part?
Yet must I leave thee, leave thee, Paradise?

STAND BY THE FLAG.

By R. Greene.

Stand by the flag! let nothing daunt
    The heart, but guard it well;
In gallant cheer we'll meet the foe,
    And make each charge to tell;
Let Honor, Pride, and Victory's wreath
    Each serve to spread the story
Of noble deeds, by British sons,
    Who fought for England's glory.

Let not the fame of bygone years
  Be lost, while yet there's blood
To brighten up old History's page,
  And make each record good;
But shout, "Britannia rules the wave,
  Victoria rules the land,"
And she expects each gallant son
  By England's flag to stand!

Stand by the flag! A traitor he
  Who'd slight the sacred trust;
An exile may he ever be,
  Who'd insult at it thrust!
But let the cry from every tongue,
  Resound o'er land and main,
"Long live Victoria, England's Queen!
  Long may Victoria reign!"

THE FEMALE AUCTIONEER.

Well, here I am; and what of that?
  Methinks I hear you cry,
For I have come, and that is pat,
  To see if you will buy.
A female auctioneer I stand,
  But not to seek for pelf,
For the only lot I've now on hand,
  Is just to sell myself.
And I'm going, going, going, going;
  Who bids—who bids for me,
For I'm going, going, going, going;
  Who bids—who bids for me.

Though some may deem me pert or so,
  They deal in idle strife;
For where's the girl, I'd like to know,
  Would not become a wife?

Indeed, I really think I should,
　　In spite of all alarms;
So, bachelors, pray be so good
　　As just take me to your arms.
　　　　For I'm going, etc.

Now, bachelors, my way towards you
　　Should not your thoughts mislead;
I've never yet been called a flirt,
　　Nor coquette, — no, indeed.
My heart and hand I offer fair,
　　And, if you buy the lot,
I vow all Caudling I will spare,
　　When Hymen ties the knot.
　　　　For I'm going, etc.

GYPSY JANE.

I'm a merry gypsy maid,
　　From my tent in yonder glade;
Selling ballads is my trade,
　　Fortunes, too, I tell.
For village maids I've comfort bland,
　　Of sweethearts who complain;
You've only got to cross the hand
　　Of little Gypsy Jane.
　　　　Tra, la, la, etc.

With the lark I greet the morn,
　　When the dew is on the rye;
With the milkmaid 'neath the thorn,
　　Stealthily am I.
For her I've tales of house and land,
　　Of husbands rich to gain;
She only has to cross the hand
　　Of little Gypsy Jane.
　　　　Tra, la, la, etc.

"ONLY WAITING."

Only waiting till the shadows
 Are a little longer grown;
Only waiting till the glimmer
 Of the day's last beam is flown;
Till the night of earth is faded
 From the heart once full of day;
Till the stars of heaven are breaking
 Through the twilight soft and gray.

Only waiting till the angels
 Open wide the mystic gate,
At whose portals I have lingered,
 Weary, poor, and desolate;
Even now I hear their footsteps,
 And their voices far away;
If they call me I am waiting,
 Only waiting to obey.

Only waiting till the shadows
 Are a little longer grown;
Only waiting till the glimmer
 Of the day's last beam is flown;
Then, far out the gathering darkness
 Holy, deathless stars shall rise,
By whose light my soul shall gladly
 Wing its passage to the skies.

———

BIRD OF BEAUTY.

Bird of beauty, whose bright plumage
 Sparkles with a thousand dyes,
Soft thy notes and gay thy carol,
 Though stern Winter rules the skies;
Soft thy notes and gay thy carol,
 Though stern Winter rules the skies.
  La, la, la, etc.

Com'st thou to mean the silence
  Of my snow-clad home to cheer,
Dost thou bear a message to me
  From the friends beloved and dear?
Dost thou bear a message to me
  From the friends beloved and dear?
        La, la, la, etc.

Where the southern roses blossom,
  By the prairie's spreading plain,
I have listened to thy warbling,
  Charméd by the magic strain;
I have listened to thy warblings,
  Charméd by the magic strain.

Welcome, for a leaf, sweet wanderer,
  Thou hast plucked and borne to me,
Bearing words of joy and gladness,
  · Mingled with sweet melody;
Bearing words of joy and gladness,
  Mingled with sweet melody.
              La, la, la, etc.

————◦◦————

THE COLD-WATER MAN.

It was an honest fisherman, —
  I knew him passing well, —
And he lived by a little pond
  Within a little dell.
A grave and quiet man was he,
  Who loved his hook and rod;
So even ran his line of life
  His neighbors thought it odd.

For science and for books, he said,
  He never had a wish;
No school to him was worth a fig,
  Except a school of fish.

He ne'er aspired to rank or wealth,
   Nor cared about a name,
For though much famed for fish was he,
   He never fished for fame.

Let others bend their necks at sight
   Of fashion's gilded wheels,
He ne'er had learned the art to bob
   For anything but eels!
A cunning fisherman was he,
   His angles all were right;
The smallest nibble at his bait
   Was sure to prove a bite!

All day this fisherman would sit
   Upon an ancient log,
And gaze into the water, like
   Some sedentary frog;
With all the seeming innocence
   And that unconscious look
That other people often wear
   When they intend to hook.

To charm the fish he never spoke,
   Although his voice was fine,
He found the most convenient way
   Was just to drop a line;
And many a gudgeon of the pond,
   If they could speak to-day,
Would own with grief this angler had
   A mighty taking way.

Alas, one day this fisherman
   Had taken too much grog,
And being but a landsman, too,
   He couldn't keep the log;
'Twas all in vain, with might and main,
   He strove to reach the shore,
Down, down he went, to feed the fish
   He'd baited oft before.

16

The jury gave their verdict that
  'Twas nothing else but gin
Had caused the fisherman to be
  So sadly taken in ;
Though one stood out upon a whim,
  And said the angler's slaughter,
To be exact about the fact,
  Was clearly gin and water.

The moral of this mournful tale
  To all is plain and clear,
That drinking habits bring a man
  Too often to his bier.
And he who scorns to take the pledge,
  And keep the promise fast,
May be, in spite of fate, a stiff
  Cold water man at last.

THE OLD CHURCH BELL.

For full five hundred years I've swung
  In my old gray turret high,
And many a different theme I've sung,
  As the time went stealing by.
I've pealed the chant of a wedding morn,
  Ere night, I've sadly tolled,
To say that the bride was coming love-lorn,
  To sleep in the churchyard mould ;
    Ding dong, my ceaseless song,
    Merry and sad, but never long.

For full five hundred years I've swung
  In my ancient turret high,
And many a different theme I've sung
  As the time went stealing by.
I've swelled the joy of a country's pride,
  For a victory far off won ;

Then changed to grief for the brave that died,
　Ere my mirth had well begun.
　　Ding dong, my ceaseless song,
　　Merry and sad, but never long.

For full five hundred years I've swung
　In my crumbling turret high;
'Tis time my own death-song were sung,
　And with truth before I die.
I never could love the theme they gave
　My tyrannized tongue to tell;
One moment for cradle, the next for grave,
　They have worn out the old church bell.
　　Ding dong, my changeful song,
　　Farewell now and farewell long.

PLYMOUTH ROCK.

'Mid the darkness and gloom of bigotry's night,
When terror and sadness and death were in sight,
A bright gleam was seen o'er the ocean's dark wave,
And the Pilgrims embarked for the land of the brave;
　For the old rock at Plymouth,
　New England's loved spot,
　Which was washed by the billows, —
　The old Plymouth Rock.

　　The wild tempest raged,
　　　'Mid the lightning's red glare,
　　And the roar of the thunder
　　　Heard awfully there;
　　The rain fell in torrents,
　　　And boisterous the wave,
　　But hope was still firm
　　　In the hearts of the brave,
　　　　As the old rock at Plymouth,
　　　　New England's loved spot, etc.

But hushed was the thunder,
  The angry waves calmed,
The forkéd lightning ceased,
  And with it the storm;
A silver light gleamed
  O'er the dark rolling wave,
And the land hove in sight, —
  'Twas the land of the brave.
    'Twas the old rock at Plymouth, etc.

They all landed safe
  On New England's loved spot,
That rock of the Pilgrims,
  The old Plymouth Rock.
When danger was o'er,
  On the dark mountain wave,
Thanksgivings were offered
  By the hearts of the brave.
    On the old rock at Plymouth, etc.

AT NIGHT'S LONE HOUR I DREAM OF HOME.

There was a place in childhood,
  That still seems dear to me,
Where oft I've lain in sweet repose,
  Beneath the shady tree.
'Twas then, in childhood's happy hours,
  I've sported blithe and gay,
And plucked the choicest of the flowers
  That in my pathway lay.

CHORUS.

Blow, blow ye gentle winds,
  Wherever I may roam,
No spot on earth I love so well
  As my own dear native home.

How lovely are the vales between
   The fair and distant hills !
All decked in nature's robes of green,
   And sparkling are the rills.
How dear, how sweet, those notes to me !—
   The sky, how bright above !
At night's lone hour I dream of thee,
   My own dear home I love.

    Blow, blow, ye gentle winds, etc.

RING THE BELL SOFTLY.

Some one has gone from this strange world of ours,
No more to gather its thorns with its flowers,
No more to linger where sunbeams must fade,
Where on all beauty death's fingers are laid.
Weary with mingling life's bitter and sweet,
Weary with parting and never to meet,
Some one has gone to the bright golden shore ;
Ring the bell softly,—there's crape on the door.

CHORUS.

Weary with mingling life's bitter and sweet,
Weary with parting and never to meet,
Some one has gone to the bright golden shore ;
Ring the bell softly,—there's crape on the door.

Some one is resting from sorrow and sin,
Happy when earth's conflicts enter not in ;
Joyous as birds, when the morning is bright,
When the sweet sunbeams have brought us their light ;
Weary with sowing and never to reap,
Weary with labor and welcoming sleep,
Some one's departed to Heaven's glad shore ;
Ring the bell softly,—there's crape on the door.

Weary with mingling life's bitter and sweet, etc.

Angels are anxiously longing to meet
One who walks with them in Heaven's bright street;
Loved ones have whispered that some one is blest,
Free from earth's trials, and taking sweet rest.
Yes! there is one more in angelic bliss,
One less to church, and one less to kiss,
One more departed to Heaven's bright shore;
Ring the bell softly, — there's crape on the door.

Weary with mingling life's bitter and sweet, etc.

SING ME THE SONG YOU USED TO SING.

MUSIC BY LESLIE.

Published by permission of G. D. Russell & Co.

Sing me the song you used to sing
  In days when I was young;
'Twill sound more sweetly now to me
  Than all that you have sung;
'Twill call me back to days of joy,
  To happy scenes of yore,
When I was but a simple child,
When I was but a simple child,
  Upon life's pleasant shore.

Oh, let the sweet, sweet strains be heard,
  The welcome notes prolong,
And happy feelings will be moved
  To echo to thy song.
Oh, let the music gently fall
  Upon my waiting ear,
And memories will hasten back,
And memories will hasten back,
  The sweet refrain to hear.

'Twill bring to mind my childhood's friends,
   Companions on life's shore;
And memories of gentle ones,
   Who walk earth's path no more.
Then let the echo of thy song,
   Come back from far-off land,
Like angel voices calling us,
Like angel voices calling us,
   To join their happy band.

HER HEART IS ALL MY OWN.

Published by permission of G. D. Russell & Co.

I wandered where the roses red
A sweet and lasting perfume shed;
Where lay the violets peeping through
The green grass, with their eyes of blue,
While over all, the birds of spring
Were softly, sweetly carolling;
Their music fell upon my ear,
And warmed my heart with precious cheer.
     Tra, la, la, etc.

But redder than the rose's hue,
More azure than the violet's blue,
Were cheeks and eyes of one I loved,
Who through the valley with me roved.
And sweeter than the robin's song,
Her warbling as we passed along,
This little maiden by my side,
Who smiled the words her lips denied.
     Tra, la, la, etc.

As down life's valley, hand in hand,
We go to reach life's final strand,
Where death's deep ocean gathers up
The joys and sorrows of earth's cup,

Her smile shall every pleasure bless,
Her voice will sing our happiness,
And though her smiles shall speak alone,
I know her heart is all my own.
　　　Tra, la, la, etc.

OFT IN THE STILLY NIGHT.

　　Oft in the stilly night,
When slumber's chain hath bound me,
　Fond memory brings the light
Of other days around me ;
The smiles, the tears of boyhood years,
　The words of love then spoken,
The eyes that shone now dimmed and gone,
　The cheerful hearts now broken !
　　Thus in the stilly night,
Ere slumber's chain has bound me,
　Sad memory brings the light
Of other days around me.

　　When I remember all
The friends so linked together,
　I've seen around me fall
Like leaves in winter weather,
I feel like one who treads alone
　Some banquet hall deserted,
Whose lights are fled, whose garlands dead,
　And all but me departed.
　　Thus in the stilly night,
Ere slumber's chain has bound me,
　Sad memory brings the light
Of other days around me.

WILL YOU COME TO MEET ME, DARLING?

When my feet have grown too weary
 Farther on to press their way,
When my spirit waits the bidding
 To be severed from its clay, .
I shall need some hand to guide me
 O'er the dark and flowing tide : —
Will you come to meet me, darling,
 When I reach the river side?

  I am here to meet you, darling,
  I am here to guide you home.

Will you leave your home of glory,
 In the mansions bright above,
And on angel wings float near me,
 Near my heart you used to love?
And all through the darkened valley
 Shall I find you by my side?
Will you come to meet me, darling,
 Will you be my angel guide?

  I am here to meet you, darling,
  I am here to guide you home.

Oh! I know the love between us
 Death can never take away;
Dearer, brighter, still it groweth,
 Near the closing of the day.
Hark! I hear the heavenly music,
 And an angel whispers, "Come!
I am here to meet you, darling,
 I am here to guide you home."

  I am here to meet you, darling,
  I am here to guide you home.

OH, SAY NOT WOMAN'S HEART IS BOUGHT.

Oh, say not woman's love is bought
  With vain and empty treasure!
Oh, say not woman's heart is caught
  By every idle pleasure!
When first her gentle bosom knows love's flame,
  It wanders never;
Deep in her heart the passion glows,
Deep in her heart the passion glows,
  She loves and loves forever!

Oh, say not woman's false as fair, —
  That like the bee she ranges,
Still seeking flowers more sweet and fair,
  As fickle fancy changes!
Ah, no! the love that first can warm
  Will leave her bosom never!
No second passion e'er can charm,
No second passion e'er can charm, —
  She loves and loves forever!

ON ROSY WINGS.

Afraid for me?
Secure and ready are my defences!
In this dark hour of night I hover round thee,
Near approaching, unknown to thee, love!
  Ye moaning breezes, around me playing,
    In pity aid me, in pity aid me.
  My sigh to him conveying!

On rosy wings of love depart,
  Bearing my heart's sad wailing,
Visit the prisoner's lonely cell,
  Console his spirit failing;

Let hope's soft whispers
　Wreathing around him,
Comfort breathing.

Recall to his fond remembrance
　Sweet visions of our love;
But let no accent reveal to him
　The sorrows, the sorrows, the griefs
My heart doth prove.
　Let no accent reveal to him
The trials I now prove,
　The sorrows, the sorrows
I prove.

———◦◦———

WHEN YOU AND I WERE YOUNG.

I love to dream of olden days,
　When you and I were young,
When happily life's golden rays
　Above our pathway hung;
And though the present brings its joy,
　To gild the passing hours,
I dream of days without alloy
　Of spring-time and its flowers, —
I live again those golden days,
　When you and I were young.

CHORUS.

Those golden days, those golden days,
When you and I were young!

I love to think of those bright hours,
　Though happy days come now;
'Tis well to prize the faded flowers
　That bloomed on youth's fair brow;
How bright the future then appeared!
　How sweetly birds then sung,

When loving friends our pathway cheered,
  When you and I were young!
I live again those golden days
  When you and I were young!
      Those golden days, etc.

The loved companions of those days
  Have left us, one by one,
And some have trod the golden ways
  To realms beyond the sun;
Yet when death's hand shall bring to view
  The scenes that hope has sung,
Oh! may we meet the friends we knew
  When you and I were young!
I live again those golden days,
  When you and I were young.
      Those golden days, etc.

HUNTING TOWER; OR, WHEN YE GANG AWA, JAMIE.

When ye gang awa, Jamie,
Far across the sea, laddie,
When ye gang to Germanie,
What will ye send to me, laddie?

I'll send ye a braw new gown, Jeanie,
The brawest in the town, lassie,
And it shall be o' silk, and gown
Wi' valenciennes set round, lassie.

That's nae gift ava, Jamie,
Silk and gowd and a', laddie,
There's ne'er a gown in a' the land
I'd like, when ye're awa, laddie.

When I come back again, Jeanie,
Frae a foreign land, lassie,
I'll bring wi' me a gallant gay,
To be your ain gude man, lassie.

Be my gude man, yoursel, Jamie,
Marry me yoursel, laddie,
And tak me ower to Germanie,
Wi' you at hame to dwell, laddie.

" I dinna ken how that wad do, Jeanie,
I dinna ken how that can be, lassie,
For I've a wife and bairns three,
And I'm no sure how ye'd agree, lassie."

———•••———

THE AMERICAN HYMN.

Published by permission of M. Keller.

Speed our Republic, O Father on high,
Lead us in pathways of justice and right;
Rulers as well as the ruled, one and all,
Girdle with virtue the armor of might!
Hail! three times hail, to our country and flag!

CHORUS.

Rulers as well as the ruled, one and all,
Girdle with virtue the armor of might!
Hail! three times hail, to our country and flag!

Foremost in battle for Freedom to stand,
We rush to arms when aroused by its call;
Still as of yore, when George Washington led,
Thunders our war cry, We conquer or fall!
Hail! three times hail, to our country and flag!

CHORUS.

Still as of yore, when George Washington led,
Thunders our war cry, We conquer or fall!
Hail! three times hail, to our country and flag!

Faithful and honest to friend and to foe,
　Willing to die in humanity's cause,
Thus we defy all tyrannical power,
　While we contend for our Union and laws!
Hail! three times hail, to our country and flag!

CHORUS.

Thus we defy all tyrannical power,
While we contend for our Union and laws!
Hail! three times hail, to our country and flag!

Rise up, proud eagle! rise up to the clouds,
　Spread thy broad wings o'er this fair Western world!
Fling from thy beak our dear banner of old,
　Show that it still is for freedom unfurled!
Hail! three times hail, to our country and flag!

CHORUS.

Fling from thy beak our dear banner of old,
Show that it still is for freedom unfurled!
Hail! three times hail, to our country and flag!

www.ingramcontent.com/pod-product-compliance
Lightning Source LLC
Chambersburg PA
CBHW030400270326
41926CB00009B/1195